# Windows down, Music On

David R Patrick

# Contents

# Dedication

I dedicate this book to all the guys on the mental health ward I shared. You may be anonymous but not to me.

To my American friend.  Someone else that had more belief in my recovery than I did.  Ian for being a friend constantly without ever making a point of it.

Stan for help with the title. A real collaboration.

Also, to my daughter for giving me hope.

Finally, to my friends, being back in my life again. Thank you.

I wish to give immense thanks to ChatGPT which is part of the OpenAI company.  ChatGPT allows me to visualise elements of this and all illustrations are from it, including the cover.

# Introduction.

"In the end, it's not the years in your life that count. It's the life in your years." -*Abraham Lincoln*

If I could have pictured the year that followed my last book, I would not have pictured this.

As for the title of this book, It reflects how I felt at the start, it is not to suggest this year was not a challenge or that whatever happened was without sadness and regret.

Overall, this was a very mixed year with a lot of ups and downs. However, I had a complete year with my brain, which was great and I start the next year even more positive than the last.

I am just going to say things as they are. It's important to me for this book, that it doesn't carry any hurt or venom. Those things are transitory and shouldn't be preserved.

Life is complicated, perspectives exist beside your own and if you know that the characters in play are good at heart, you have to have space to allow their side of a story and possible intentions. It is easy to just see your own, even though you know there are always two.

When things take a turn for the worse, it may be difficult to remember that but its important. The reason I love writing so much, is it makes you face these sorts of issues.

Saying that, hopefully you know me by now, the light always shines stronger for me and attracts me more than the draw of the dark and that reflects in this book.

I should also say that all statements made in this book are based on what I have seen, experienced and read about and cannot be seen to reflect on the whole Mental Health service. Although they can be seen as indicative and many trusts, including this one often make the press because of it.

It is very important to note that none of the illustrations are real, or based on real people. They are purely meant to convey how I felt at the time, which they do very well for me.

# Chapter 1

I never considered the possibility that getting my brain back could turn out to be a mixed blessing. However, as you will find out, dear reader it truly was.

They say what a difference a year makes. After my previous several years recovering from brain damage, I was kind of hoping for a year just catching up on all that I missed. Little did I know that was not meant to be. When we were together last, it was right around the very last stages of my recovery and I wrote the book as I tried to make sense of what had happened.

I feel this will be a similar experience. I have analysed certain parts of the last year so many times and other parts not at all. Well, if you are in for this ride, so am I. It has proven to be eventful.

I feel I have dealt with this a lot better than I would have done because of the changes in my character that have occurred from the recovery. I now have this overriding sense that what will be, will be and I am much calmer in that.

# Chapter 2

My wife and I started corresponding via email, in early 2001, during a period after I had broken an ankle and had to work from home for several weeks.

I had always loved Japanese food, culture, architecture and art. In fact, I was interested in almost all aspects of Japan. I have always been somewhat of a traveller since reaching the age of 18. When I was young, we only ever went on one holiday that I can remember, which was in the same county. I developed a real taste for travel that once I could organise it for myself, I sated on it.

I have spent quite a large part of my life travelling the world and negotiated a deal with work at one time, where each year I took six weeks out to travel around the world, which were my main holidays all combined.

I did six of those round the world trips. I even built some software, to allow me to plan unusual routes on the airline alliances.

My wife had always loved the UK and took her annual one week leave (that's all she got in Japan) and had travelled to the UK to visit the Scottish Highlands and the Lake District. Places on my own doorstep I haven't seen.

She had taken time out and lived for a few months in Leeds and Newcastle to study English.

Japan had this really sweet cultural pen pal site (Pen Pal… there is a word you don't see anymore). We started corresponding by email. I had a lot of time on my hands, because of my ankle, without the ability to go anywhere and I used that time to write to my wife whenever I could. We wrote to each other every day and then progressed to speaking via phone.

We became fairly besotted, we each built up phone bills of several hundred pounds a month, for months on end, talking for hours every day. These were the days before Whats App and Skype and before telecoms operators offered bargain fixed price international calls.

My wife came to visit and we spent a week around Windsor, which was really nice and by the time my wife had to go home, we had decided to move in together. Probably the wisest move of my life.

My wife travelled over on September 11th 2001, in the middle of a typhoon in Tokyo. Her plane was one of the only planes to land at Heathrow the following morning, given the atrocity taking place in another city.

We were married the following year, both locally in England and in a ceremony in Japan. My wife was a talented well-known hairdresser in Japan. She worked locally in a hairdressing salon in the area, when she first moved over.

Our daughter was born in the summer of 2006 and we have treasured our time with her since. She is gifted academically and also artistically in all regards. She can sing, dance, adores drama and art in all forms and her natural skill definitely did not emanate from me or my side of the family.

My wife's father was a talented musician and my wife is incredible with crafts, so I can see where her artistic side comes from.

As my daughter entered junior school my wife started working at the same school and has ever since. She is a natural with children, she works hard, is liked a lot by the children and people like working with her because of her work ethic and constant positivity to her work.

In our twenty years together my wife and I never even argued that I can remember once, I don't ever remember raising my voice with her and we both adored our daughter. I loved my wife and daughter with the love that is sure you will be together in the after-life, as well as this, if there is one that is.

My daughter from the age of 2 was reticent with anything new. She watched and studied others before trying new things. We soon realised that she was making sure it was safe before she tried things and she had her own understanding of any dangers.

My daughter has been gifted at school. We have never had to chase her on her homework and she naturally drove herself to achieve. She had a natural sense of competitiveness, although she never bragged and she had done exceptionally well despite not being tutored, which is very rare in a modern grammar school.

I loved my family and we enjoyed our life. However, as I have learnt, things can change and you don't always see them coming.

# Chapter 3

As I mentioned in my previous book, the final stages of my recovery all came together over a fairly short period. Looking back, I can see that I acquired most of my logic and processing capability first and then, the things I gained towards the end were interaction skills, verbal communication skills, debating skills and more advanced expression skills and then came the ability to deal with wider ranges of situations.

That may not be exact. But the fundamentals of being able to think, consider, organise, problem solve and rationalise maybe took 5 years. The fundamentals of how to interact and deal with people maybe a year and then everything else was in less than six months.

Since I was a young programmer (shows my age, people were not called coders then), even though I was only a programmer for a few years, I once completely lost a key program I had been working on for days and had not taken backups. Since then, I am what you would politely call overly cautious.

I save a new version name, on any documents I am working on (including books), every hour or so and therefore generate a lot of versions, when I look back at my first book, it quite clearly shows when the book was predominantly written and when most changes had occurred, based on the date and times of the versions of the book.

I was writing the book until the end of January and the events of this book start maybe a week later. For me during the later stages of my recovery, the way I thought developed rapidly.

Right around the time that I needed the interaction with people, on a regular basis every day, I would find that my cognitive ability developed on a regular basis and in some cases the way I thought through things, changed from the way I was before 2015.

For example, if I had a problem to solve, I found I could think about it, then get on with something else and the answer would pop up at a later stage (like I had sent the problem off for processing and then got notified of the results). Some of these changes stuck and others didn't. This one didn't.

I believe this was probably all to do with the way my brain was rebuilding itself and the neurons reconnecting. If I ever find out definitively, I will update this. What I do know is, when the vocabulary literally flooded back at the end (so disconcerting), somehow, I was aware of this.

This also happened with memories. As I spoke to people about subjects for a while, sometimes hundreds of memories would flood back. Again, I would suddenly be aware of this. For me this must have been final connections being made to old memories in clusters.

This only happened at the end of my recovery but at that time it happened a lot and quickly.

Overall, I actually feel my abilities to problem solve are even better than they used to be and the same with many other cognitive skills. When writing for example I find my writing flows to the paper with less effort and in a more natural way.

Additionally, I think I find the ability to generate ideas on any subject easier than before. It's a strange one, trying to compare these things but it really does seem to be that way.

I was happy, if disorientated by the changes as I knew that I was getting skills back I hadn't had since before my illness. However, it was clear sometimes that these new skills were unnerving to my wife and maybe also my daughter.

My wife is very perceptive about many things although very self-deprecating of her abilities. She told me that as I got very busy my speech patterns often changed and I spoke faster.

My speech had been very modulated since I stopped working because my brain had been very limited in what it had been called to do. It was as if, when I became myself again and I started doing more, this speed increase in my voice automatically occurred.

It was interesting because until my wife mentioned it, I didn't notice it and at the time I couldn't tell whether I was speaking fast.  After a day or so and being aware it may happen, it stopped happening but it was clear it had unnerved her.

This is the first in a series of things I have analysed many times.  I think she saw similarities with the manic episode of 2015 and interpreted whether consciously or unconsciously, my fast speech in this instance, as reminiscent of that mania.

I assured her at the time, that instead this was me recovering my mental cognitive skills and that once aware of the problem, immediately I could control my speech just by stopping working, and taking a few minutes out.  When I was manic there was no off switch and all my patterns of thought were affected.

I did kind of recognise this may be disorientating but I must have massively underestimated it.

We had a series of moments after I recovered, where we tried to touch on elements of what happened in 2015 and in the six and a half years that followed.  I had waited until I had fully recovered, as I felt if I didn't, opening this can of worms could only make things worse. However, anything that touched the subject of my mania and what followed, led to my wife getting extremely upset and breaking out in tears.  It felt to me like a form of PTSD.

My wife made it clear to me, she didn't want to ever read the book I had written, despite the fact that it would explain everything that had happened to me. In our limited discussions it was clear to me, it was because she could not stand to open those wounds.

At one point in the next week, she asked me to read a bit from the book, in what would be a final attempt to see if she would be able to read the book and within 30 seconds we had to stop. I had actually chosen a section with a light story in it but it still obviously hurt.

Looking back on it now, I believe that my wife saw in all my signs of rapid recovery, instead a trigger link to what had happened in 2015 and just couldn't see past that.

Even though I had always been excited and passionate about everything I do, I just don't think she could look past the perceived link to the rapid speech and the sudden ability to think clearly and quickly again, to the episode of mania several years before, and my reasoning for that will soon become clear.

I had some excellent, thought-provoking discussions with my daughter who at 15 at the time displayed greater cognitive skills than many post-grads I mentored. One evening we spent hours in a discussion.

This was silly on my part as after our first really deep discussion, my daughter got so excited, she didn't sleep properly all night. This in itself must have been extremely disorientating for her. After so many years where we had never had a deep conversation as I was incapable of it, we had the deepest conversation we had ever had (but then she had just turned 9 when I fell ill).

My wife was rightly extremely concerned by this and we agreed that any such conversations should be held much earlier in the day to not affect her sleep.

In my being physically present for so many years but absent in mind, my wife had taken over the mantel of parenting for both of us. For much of that time I was incapable of input and for much longer incapable of communicating, what I wanted to say clearly or effectively.

So, I limited it and my wife managed this. I would say well done to my daughter for all her high grades and so forth but for obvious reasons she didn't look to me for direction.

In what follows, I will just state what happened and make my best guess for those things I don't know. Since I don't know both sides, I will do my best not to cast judgement, as there are always two sides to a story and it is not fair to cast judgement without hearing both.

Additionally, my wife was one of the nicest people I knew in the world, so what appeared to happen is likely to have much more behind it. What I need to do here, is to give her the benefit of the doubt. That seems only fair.

I do remember my wife telling me quite early in our relationship, that people mistake the Japanese for nice. As she once said, the trouble is people see politeness as being nice. However, in Japan everything is beneath the surface.

However, in everything I had ever seen of her, she cared a lot. In her work at a junior school, she did much more than was expected and I have never known her to be nasty to anyone.

That all seems very vague. Don't worry it will all become clear shortly.

What happens next, in regards to my daughter, I have looked at and thought on many, many times and think it was probably purely the result of us not being able to **really** talk for so long and for me to suddenly be dealing with an extremely intelligent and very determined young lady, rather than a young daughter.

I hadn't realised, as we hadn't spoke on this but my wife had developed a way of talking about what had happened and our current lives, that protected my daughter from any concerns. All very understandable.

The trouble was I was unaware of this and mentioned something that was a trigger for my daughter, money.  Since I hadn't been working things were more constricted, although we never went completely without, and I was purely trying to say I wanted to find a way for my wife and daughter to be able to go on holiday to Japan again.  They had gone annually until I fell ill.

My daughter got extremely upset and ran up to her room.  I tried to placate her but we hadn't built that rapport yet.

I had never had a disagreement with my daughter or wife before, if I knew what was happening, I would have avoided it.  I knew my wife hated confrontation or disagreements of any kind.

In this situation it escalated.   I wanted my daughter to understand my point of view, my wife didn't want to have an argument with me in any way, yet wanted to protect my daughter.

My daughter may well have been taken aback as this sort of discussion we hadn't had before. My wife listened, didn't say anything, which I assumed at the time was because she wasn't going to take a position between myself and my daughter.

From my perspective, having regained my faculties, I just wanted my daughter to acknowledge me.  I think it was me just wanting to be treated as an adult again after all the years, where I really wasn't part of the familial structure.  However I know that these things have to be earnt not imposed but at the time, well I didn't think of that.

The reality is this whole thing didn't matter.  I tried to stop this escalating but it didn't work.  I think back now and wonder if I raised my voice.  I may have.  I don't remember.

I look back and think that, all that was needed was time for us to have talked, for me to get know the way of the land again and to be used to using my faculties again.  I am a very quick learner.

I have thought about this a lot and for me it is quite difficult. When I came back after brain injury, I was really enthusiastic, that after all this time and the endless repetition, trying to awake my brain for many years, I was actually me again.  I had escaped my locked cage. One I had imagined I was consigned to for ever.

I immediately wanted to change things, to show I would make up for my failures to be able to do anything whilst I was gone. I had the enthusiasm back from when I was myself before.

Within days of becoming myself, I started work on my first book to document it (although originally targeted at friends and family). I threw myself into the task as this would allow me to reconnect with people.

As discussed in my last book, I started contacting old friends. This was at the same time. Until that point the only phone calls I took were from Ian and my brother over many years. I was suddenly on phone calls for a number of hours a day. I used to laugh a lot, was quite loud before I was ill and I was like that again.

When I think back over those several years I was recovering, I don't really remember me laughing, not a hearty laugh that you lose yourself to. Suddenly I was having those conversations that made me laugh out loud. For a house quiet to such sounds for so long, it must have been very disconcerting for my wife and daughter.

I was trying to work out my way forward in terms of friendship etc. For people that hadn't seen or spoken to me for many years this may have been too much. I hadn't really thought that when someone has been gone so long and you have no idea why, maybe you don't care as much when they suddenly arrive back on the scene.

Maybe it was like a sudden reboot of Happy Days. People had moved on. Anyway, I am normally a very accommodating guy and I generally think more from everyone else's perspective. In fact, I always used to say to people when talking about situations, "see the world through their eyes but with what you know"

In arguments I always used to see the other side. When I came back it took me a few weeks to find myself again in a balanced way with so many changes occurring, as I was so keen to be back and a mind craving interaction. So, I don't think in these early weeks as I navigated my own brain, that I was performing the fine art of considering anyone else's position. In fact, I know I wasn't. Trying to manage the final changes in me was a full-time job. The net effect would have been though, I would definitely have seemed less considerate.

It also took a few weeks for others to get used to me. I can be quite immediate and full on, especially as I was just so happy to be back and be able to interact with these people after so long and whilst all these people were really good friends before they hadn't dealt with me for many years. For most the last they saw me or knew of me was in the mental health wards before I cut links.

Obviously, the book helped a lot (probably more difficult for those who didn't read it and some people just don't read books). However, I hadn't thought of the way it might feel, if you simply had moved on. Hi its me, I know it's been 7 years but read my book and can we chat.

I have six friends I am now in regular contact with but looking back it was much rockier re-establishing contact with people than it would ever normally be.  At the time I was expecting people to understand my position and accommodate it.

For me you see, I had spent those years when I could think at all hoping one day, I would re-establish contact with these friends.

Anyway, I was less aware of everyone's feelings, as so much was happening to me.  As such some of the people I cut contact with I was probably being harsh on.  Actually, I was harsh on, if I judge it against how I am normally (both before illness and after recovery).

I was also quite "I'm here again" and just suddenly back full throttle with my brother and sister.  We had always accommodated each other and during this period it was my full attention, full on.  Which just isn't the way we deal with each other.  I had always been low key with both my brother and sister.

My sister thought I was a programmer in a letter she wrote to the DWP in 2016.  I was last a programmer in 1987.  So you can tell  we didn't really go into the detail of what I did for work on a regular basis.  Suffice it to say things got very difficult between myself, my sister and my brother during those weeks.

I had expectations that on seeing my recovery, I would have this sudden, massive support from my family and it just wasn't like that. We had never really been like that before so I don't know why I thought that.

I managed to repair bridges with my brother but not my sister. In fact me and my brother, who lives abroad speak more regularly now, than I remember in the last 20 years.

With my daughter I had tried to filter everything that was happening but with my wife, I was trying to explain everything that was happening and I think that difference mattered. I had always told my wife what was going on and given the sheer significance of the changes and my recovery, I could only see the positive side. The same was not true I think for my wife.

The weird thing was this period was fleeting and was just coming to an end, though some of its results not. Within days my brain reached the end of its changes, its impact on me settled.

All of the above must have affected my wife. It was so sudden and so immediate, maybe the other things were too much for my wife, who was still very fragile re the events of 2015. The next morning everything changed, perhaps forever.

# Chapter 4

This is a bewildering day for me which will become clear as time goes on.  At this point I knew that my daughter was still upset with me, I really was looking for her to apologize and my wife was avoiding the subject, which at the time I thought was just not wanting to get involved.

Me and my wife had a long conversation (maybe 45 minutes) about how an old school friend of my daughter was cutting herself, had been taken out of school and was being taught from home.  My wife said that the girl's pet rats had died and my daughter was going there to comfort her and to help with her homework.  She was taking the rats with her as well to comfort her.  She also mentioned that she and my daughter had bagged up a lot of old clothes and would be taking them to the charity shop.  It was a very positive conversation.

I talked about how proud I was of my daughter for doing such a good thing.

We had a washing machine being fitted that morning and an old friend I hadn't spoken to for several years, called just as they were leaving.  I said goodbye and they went.

I spoke to my friend for 2-3 hours.  We both used to make each other laugh a lot and the time flew by. Almost as soon as I put the phone down, I had got a text.  It was from my wife.

It basically said that my wife couldn't cope, she needed to look after her mental health, she was staying with a friend. Goodbye.

There hadn't been an argument, though my wife had been upset about my disagreement with my daughter, she had cried a number of times discussing the events of my recovery, she had been worried by my speech patterns.  I just couldn't see these as the reason why a 20-year marriage would break down, especially without a discussion.

I wracked my brain as to what else it was but at the time, I didn't think there was enough to drop 20 years of marriage without a conversation and to take my daughter away from the only home she had known.

Looking at it now, I can only assume that these triggers worried her much more than I understood, that she somehow believed they were indications of a return of a manic phase and couldn't cope with the idea of a reoccurrence.

Of course, there are lots of other reasons people leave a marriage which could be possible but it would be unfair to assume as there had been no indication at all of other parties involved.  In the future I will update when I know the full facts, if I ever do know the full facts.

Although I have indicated other reasons, it's only to show I am not naïve and I considered every option, I could sensibly think of.  From now I will focus on trying to give my wife representation in this.  As I have said, It doesn't mean I haven't considered other things; I just don't think it's fair to ignore her side of the story, which for reasons that will become clear is not accessible to me.

I realised in searching through my memory of our conversations of the previous days looking for any clues, my wife had told me in the middle of a discussion, regarding someone at school that she had a disagreement with, about how she hated confrontation or disagreement of any kind.

That may well have been her trying to explain why she did what she did, in the way that she did it.

Anyway, whilst I may be generally calm about these things, I am not a robot, she was the love of my life and my daughter the apple of my eye. I had just got them back (in the sense I was just back). In fact, they were the reason I had never given up.

What followed was a desperate attempt for me to find out what the hell was going on. Was it she didn't love me anymore, had she met someone else, was it that she wanted to be on her own.

It wasn't pretty as I would guess it isn't for anyone who doesn't see it coming and believes that they were with the love of their life. Taking my daughter as well only felt like someone had kicked dirt in my face.

I won't go into this period but you can imagine, it is like dealing with the 7 stages of grief in a couple of hours. I tried everything I could, not to necessarily change her mind but to understand why it had happened.

When it happens without explanation, it is like losing someone without knowing what happened to them. The event itself is seismic, the not knowing is just pouring iodine in the wounds (that really, really hurts by the way). That evening I realised that my wife had taken the majority of her clothes and most of my daughter's clothes, so it became obvious this wasn't a getting away from it for a few days to think.

One other thing, my wife's long speech in the morning was obviously a cover. Together me and my wife had helped one of her friends get away from an abusive husband only literally a month or so before and the more I looked at it the more it seemed like the sort of cover story you would give in those circumstances.

Maybe my wife had really been affected by these triggers to what she may have saw as reminiscent of 2015 and that was the reason. Whatever it was it must have worried her though with all the time I spent going through it I couldn't see it at the time.

Little did I know that things were about to get a lot worse.

# Chapter 5

I invited my friend Ian around.  I told him what had happened and he was convinced it must be a mistake of some kind.  However, he came round.  This is the same guy that was always there for me during my recovery.

This was a couple of hours after my text message and after I realised that my seven stages of grief messages would not elicit a response of any kind.

We had a few drinks and he was just dumbstruck by what happened and convinced it would blow over.

On one of my messages, I had told my wife that given I was the main insurance holder and the car was in my name, that unless we could talk, I would cancel the insurance and road tax.  My wife left the car on the road and me and my friend moved it to my drive.

I should say, my wife had been in a car accident a few months before and written off two cars (thankfully everyone was OK), I was unsure of how she was and yes of course I also wanted a reason to talk to her about what had happened.

I then saw I had got a message, from of all people in the world the mental health crisis team.  The people I had said were the last people in the world I ever wanted to see.

Looking at positive intentions, If my wife really mistook my recovering cognitive function for indicators of the return of mania, then she may well have thought she was acting in my best interests.

As to how I know it was my wife, that had contacted them. Ian was the only other person that knew my wife had left me and they mentioned about whether I considered life worth living.

In my 7 stages of grief, right about the shock stage, I did send messages that said the reason I saw for my existence was my wife and my daughter and questioned whether life was worth living without them. However, that stage lasted for about 5 minutes and I imagine that most men devoted to their family would express something like that, early on.

My focus in my messages was really all about what had I done wrong, why had she left me, why after 20 years couldn't she tell me, whether If I did something I could change it (I would have), whether I hadn't communicated enough or showed enough, I would do anything I could to preserve our marriage and family. How could I communicate with her (I wasn't getting any messages back)

However, this referral was enough for the Mental Health Crisis Team, who took that statement at face value and contacted me. I then had to spend 2 hours on the phone less than 4 hours after my wife had left me, trying to convince them that I was OK, considering my wife of 20 years had just left me and taken my daughter.

The woman on the phone enquired as to whether I was taking abilify, from the single incident I had seven years before, in 2015. The fact is during that one prolonged mania period I was let go way too early (as soon as my wife was back in the country after being with her mum as she died) and had to go back into the unit within days, meant they classified my problem as a recurring ongoing issue and considered me in remission, despite only that one major crisis in my life. As such they expected me to still be taking abilify 7 years later.

I offered for her to speak to my friend who told her I was OK. However, knowing the Mental Health Services Team, I told my friend that tomorrow I would have a knock on the door. He told me categorically, no way on earth. I went to bed fearing the worst for the next day. Sometimes you don't want to be proved right.

# Chapter 6

As you can imagine, I didn't sleep that well, that night.  A combination of worrying about what I could have done to cause my wife to leave with my daughter and what would happen next i.e., what would she do.

I also had what I knew would be a problem with the Mental Health Crisis team becoming involved.  Some time is needed for background.

The mental health crisis team, is as it sounds the NHS services that step in,  when they believe that someone is in crisis and specifically where they may be of danger to themselves or others.

The thing with this team.  If you go to them in crisis, there is virtually no chance that they will do anything for you.  They have to make the decision to engage.

So, in the following chapters, I want you to consider that whilst this happened to me, some people have literally been at their door for months and the crisis team will refuse to engage.  In one case close to home the results of that were tragic.

However, for me within hours of my wife reporting it, despite it being a Saturday and me only once in my life being ill, I was top of their list.  Sometimes you don't want to be wanted in this way.

Now, bear in mind in the following my wife had unexpectedly left me, less than 4 hours before they called (when I got the text) and 6 hours by the time, I had managed to get them on the phone.

I then had to spend two hours discussing this with them to convince them I was OK and even passed them over to a friend to speak to.

From the notes (obtained under GDPR) in which the Mental Health caller wrote that I seemed calm and pleasant and returned the call to "reassure I was safe and well" but was sad (their choice of descriptive words). They wrote that my friend did not see or have any concerns.

You would think that would be that then.  I mean surely anyone realises, people will be a little upset on the day their wife of 20 years leaves without a word and takes their child, they may be a little upset.

# Chapter 7

Once the crisis team call you, if you have piqued their interest, the next day regardless of day of the week, they may well doorstep you and the following day they could be assessing you for admission and from there, they can take you directly to hospital for assessment. They offer you the choice of voluntary admission and if you say no, they take you under section i.e., legally and if needed forcefully.

When people are in crisis, this no-nonsense approach is often needed to deal quickly with situations where people are a danger to themselves or others.

I knew regardless of the call (I didn't have the notes at this stage but knew it was all very pleasant), that I may only have one and a half days to get things done as I knew all conversations with mental health, will be about me taking abilify.

Fundamentally if labelled a recurring issue and once a prescription has been determined,  all future conversations really are just about you taking the drug, if you no longer are.  If you refuse, then the rest of the conversation is about mounting evidence for you to be assessed, so that you can be assigned the drug, under section if necessary.

If you read my previous book, you will know why that was a no no. I got the locks changed that next morning and started to arrange to sell the car, knowing my time was probably limited.

However, after thinking through what I could have done to cause my wife to leave and what my wife was thinking, I realised I would have to switch modes, as my time would be limited before I would be taken in for an assessment. I started instead thinking what is this all about and what would she be doing next.

I did a quick search to get an understanding of what had been taken by my wife and I was shocked. As well as almost all clothes, it was most of the essentials (all toiletries, soaps, gels, shampoos, makeup etc), all legal documents related to my wife and daughter including passports etc, all schoolbooks for my daughter. Wherever I looked, I noticed more had been taken. For example, 500 sheets of printer paper were taken, which took me back.

I started thinking what is the worst that can happen that I need to act on as it was clear not only were they not coming back but my wife had planned for the long term.

My daughter is dual nationality. She can choose up to the age of 21 to switch nationality to Japanese. Japan does not allow dual passports, so to do so you give up British nationality.

The short version is that parental abduction to Japan is common and Japan does not extradite as per the Hague convention if the mother and child are Japanese nationals.

I phoned the police as I has seen on metropolitan police web sites that in these cases an all-ports alert can be put out to stop one of the parents leaving the country with the child.

I wasted some time as the first police officer I spoke to, stated that I had no rights as a parent stopping my wife leaving the country with our child who was under 16.  I explained I did and referred her to police advice sites on the same but no joy.

I called back and spoke to a supervising officer and this was then overridden and an all-ports alert was put out on my wife and daughter.  I will say I complained to the police about the behaviour of the officer giving incorrect advice about such a critical subject and to their credit, the police force arranged extra training for all 999 staff on this and for it to be added to handbooks for the future.

Anyway, once the police got into gear, they really stepped it up and I was fielding many calls from 999 while they investigated the circumstances.

At this time the doorbell went and my heart sank.  It was a mental health team who wanted to come in to talk to me.  I explained that the police were issuing an all-ports alert and I was receiving constant calls from them (I got one from 999 at that point and showed them) but they would not come back and doorstepped their way in.

What followed was a bit farcical.  The police called and asked me to check things, for example on one call was whether there were any joint accounts, had money been moved in the last few days between key accounts, had anything of mine been taken.

The stream of calls was about every 10 minutes or more, they would ask me to check things and either they would have called back for an update or I would call and update them.

As soon as the phone was put down, I was subject to a barrage of questions from the mental health team.  Even when I explained that I was doing things for the police from the 999 line, they would constantly interrupt.  One of the Crisis team said that "police issues had nothing to do with them".

In all of this I didn't think or know my wife would leave the country with my daughter.  It was less than 24 hours since she left and she had told me nothing.  At the identical time she went invisible on WhatsApp the same happened with my daughter (it was coordinated) and I was ghosted on other platforms.  She had taken all the documents to go abroad and I had no idea of her intent.

I was just worried she would leave and using a common-sense risk approach you say how likely is it (and that was unknown but definitely possible) and what is the impact (well once they were there, that was the end of it), I knew it was a risk I didn't want to take and the police agreed.

One of the crisis team said I seemed a bit agitated.  I explained yet again: Wife of 21 years suddenly left with just a text message, she had taken my daughter, less than 24 hours but had taken all legal documents, Hague convention doesn't apply in Japan, All Ports Alert being issued etc. Nothing, they just blanked that and said that's a police matter, nothing to do with us.  The next conversation abilify.

I explained one incident in my life, 7 years ago. Took drugs for 2 years, no memory of those years.  No other occurrence before or after. Again, I saw blank looks.  I was told in no uncertain terms, take the drugs or you will be going to the assessment unit.

I told them about my book, which explained my experiences and I offered for them to look at the copy of the manuscript I had with me but they refused. I mention this as both the refusal (If they refuse to look at a book say, they can still call you delusional about its existence) and when they blank you (if they do not answer or acknowledge you, they can feign they didn't hear it and they can exclude anything you say, that is not in alignment with their determined perspective).

I noticed throughout my conversations with Mental Health Services, including when in hospital about these tricks of ignoring what you say and not "seeing" proof of anything, when it's convenient.  It's so endemic, it looks at face value to me as though it is either taught or shared.

You combine this with refusing the recording of calls (you are entitled to record them, regardless of what they say as per BMJ guidance). Any medical consultation regarding yourself can be recorded. What I learnt is that most mental health staff do not want a record taken of what has happened.

Given that normally people are ill and the above, this leads some people to abuse their positions and the powers they are given. For me luckily some meetings have multiple people and dedicated note takers, that record what you actually said...

I should explain that in my experience, quite a number of people in this crisis unit come across as bullies, arrogant, patronising and act as though they hold your life in their hands (to an extent they do). They seem to enjoy intimidating people.

I will take a step back for a moment. A lot of people do not realise the power that these mental health crisis teams have over you. Many people don't realise you cannot ignore them or refuse to meet with them.

If you do, they just escalate and it happens rapidly. As mentioned, the standard route to an assessment unit is a phone call, a face-to-face meeting then a formal mental health act assessment. If you are unlucky, all three could take place in 24 hours and you will be on your way to an institution by then.

If you refuse to meet, the next time the crisis team will be with the police and can literally turn up 24/7 (when I was very ill, they turned up on my doorstep at around midnight).

They can gain entry to your house without permission and can take you by force if needed to a safe place.

When I was ill, I was kind of oblivious to the detail of what was happening to me. When I distributed my first book to friends and family, one of my friends said that some areas were covered less than they had wanted.

An example was about the mental health assessment unit. The reason for this was because of how ill I was, I had limited memories of my time there. I had however taken notes for a while when I first entered the unit. This I am sure was also impacted by the medication I was taking given my later memory losses.

As I was aware of the process for the team from before, I asked to record the conversation in every conversation I had. As the process was happening quite fast and I was also on a schedule to get other things done, I hadn't researched this. This is a massive regret.

In every meeting people refused to allow me to record the conversation. I said I thought I had rights. They just flat out refused. We do actually have the rights to record the conversation with one party consent for all doctor patient conversations.

From BMJ "It is not uncommon for patients to ask to record consultations and they don't need a doctor's consent to do so. Under data protection regulations the information in the recording belongs to them and they have the right to use it as they choose.".

Since I was very ill in 2015, when I came out, all I wanted to do was be back home with no reminders of my time in the unit. However, this time apart from my circumstances I was absolutely fine. What shocked me was that didn't seem to affect things… all they wanted to know was would I take the medication. When I said I no they said if you don't take it, you are going to the assessment unit. As they left, they told me it would be later that day I would have the formal assessment.

I have never liked bullies and was shocked that it was obvious that regardless of what I said, I was going to end up in assessment. A catch 22 to end them all. I can go willingly or be taken away.

What I later found out truly shocked me and I will discuss in much more detail later. Many months later I received under GDPR a copy of the notes of this meeting. I was staggered. What was written by them bore no relation to reality at all. For the moment just remember these two will later be called the infamous two.

One of the things, I will mention now is that the team had to write 3 documents. Two were requests for an AMHP for a mental health act assessment (they were different layout forms but the same general questions so I am assuming they were for different departments).

Each wrote to one. On one stunning outrageous claims were made that I was seeing evil in people and that I believed a car had been stolen despite it being on my drive.

I was actually selling the car (had a quote before our meeting and one an hour after, I sold it the next day and it was picked up the following morning). I have proof of all of these.

The second is actually both vindictive and nasty.  I was let out early in 2015 and my wife was back from just burying her mother and with her father due to die.  This was obviously an incredible burden on both my wife and daughter.  To release me unwell in these circumstances, very questionable.  The net effect I couldn't support my wife, in the worst moments of her life and the whole situation made me even worse.

When I went back, I had a thing about good and evil, heaven and hell.  What no one seemed to think of, was I was placed back in a situation where my wife was consumed with grief with recent and imminent family deaths surrounding us and no one thought it may be connected.  It seems now quite obvious why my illness should suddenly encompass these things.

Anyway, it was raised as a single question "did I see evil in people" (normally there are a barrage of similar questions) and I stated unequivocally, that this was not the case.  What is most shocking is that someone would lie like this and not even bother to corroborate their story with the person sitting next to them.

I assume that they think that ill people will never read the documentation held about them.  I certainly hadn't when I was ill.  This was the start of it.  I realised later it was endemic in the trust.  What I also realised is once they take a position, they just look for evidence to support that given position as the easy path, quoting earlier notes from other people's documents, as though they themselves had witnessed it.

At that stage I just decided to switch tacks. I wasn't going to be able to avoid going to assessment, they were not listening to what I said, so as we always did at work, I disrupted the approach.

I phoned them and said, let's do it, I have packed and I am ready to go, I will write about the services that you provide and how you approach them, I will put them in a book and treat this as a busman's holiday with the government covering all costs.

This really unnerved the people in the crisis team, I spoke to. I was meant to have an assessment they said, I couldn't say I wanted to go. I phoned them several times that day to ask when the assessment was going to happen. I was told it could be up to 11pm. No-one arrived.

I also investigated who I reported concerns on the process with (the CQC) and the trusts complaints email. I posted comments against set Facebook and twitter posts on my MP's and the Mental Health Services Minister, where I wanted a record of these e.g., where I was unhappy with the way that the trust had approached these meetings and the disregard to my circumstances.

I also took key notes and just stated to my MP that I wanted to keep them up to date. The reason I did this.

- a public record timestamped by Facebook and Twitter,
- a downloadable record of the same
- that if investigated the MP and Mental Health services Minister would be able to verify, what I had said (and their IT department when it occurred).

# Chapter 8

I used my time to send a copy of my book to my MP and the Mental Health Minister, arrange for extra locks to be fitted first thing the next morning and I sold the car and arranged for it to be picked up the next day.

I still had no idea when I would be assessed (I had been bounced around overnight to various councils, none of which it turned out had anything to do with the process).

However, I found out my wife had contacted my landlord, informed them that she was leaving and stated that I may be leaving too. Obviously, she was aware that I may also be going in for assessment (and I was lucky I hadn't already).

We had been living here at that time for 16 years and being in assessment for an unknown time could have made the situation quite dire. It was the first time my wife had contacted the landlord directly; it was always me that organised extensions etc.

I had said to my wife that I was terminating the lease. This was so it could be put in my name going forward. I did say in the initial minutes/hours that I didn't know what I was going to do as I was completely thrown.

Anyway, the situation was resolved. I had told my wife I had changed the keys and she was also contacting them to see if she could get access to a copy.

At this stage I could only see that my wife left, she told the landlord, she wanted access to the property while I was "detained" based on what she had said (I didn't know what that was). At that stage I did not see a caring side to what she was doing.

Looking back, it may well have been, that she wanted to make sure she had no liability going forward with the property and didn't consider the repercussions.

I recontacted a locksmith and arranged locks for all the remaining access locks to the property. I also ordered additional window locks (I already had them but put secondary locks on all the main windows).

At this stage my wife didn't respond to me at all on Whats App but I realised she was reading the messages.

About Midday a team arrived to assess me. This was no ordinary assessment team. The Psychiatrist was the same psychiatrist that had come 7 years before, there was a nurse from the ward I was on 7 years before as well as 2 other staff. No one from the crisis team was in attendance.

I knew this was unusual (a lot of effort) but the question was why?

I was told I could not record the conversation. I made clear that ultimately, I had been told, that unless I acquiesced and decided to take Abilify, I would be going to the assessment unit.

I gave a copy of my book to one of the assessors and he thumbed through it for several minutes (this was the AMHP). I also showed emails from Mind (to who I had offered the book to for free) and from my MP's office (who had acknowledged receipt of the book).

We discussed the situation for 30-40 minutes and I made clear that whereas I had been ill in 2015, this time the only thing for me was sadness in my circumstance.  I made clear I would not be taking abilify in any scenario and outlined why.

I said that if it was necessary for them to assess me in order to be convinced that I was OK, then I would do that and use the time to document the system and write a book about my experiences.

They (across the board) gave me no indication throughout that they saw any reason for me to have to go for assessment.

At the end of the conversation, the thing that mattered most to them was that I would not take abilify.  They said that as I was willing to go for an assessment voluntarily they would arrange this.  They said that they were not considering this urgent and that it maybe a number of days before I was admitted.

Little did I know that the mandatory legal forms, required for admittance to hospital for assessment were never completed.  I was not told this. I requested my records, many months later.  The legal document was not in the several hundred pages supplied.  I asked where the document was.  After pursuing this for a month I received a letter from the trust.

In it they stated that the legally required report was not in the database. The letter stated that in these circumstances the report would be filed with the supervisor who would file it at a later date but that did not happen.

When questioned the AMHP believed he didn't write a legally required report, when asked why he didn't know. There was a process for identifying when a document wasn't filed but it didn't find this. In a search of all AMHP reports mine was the only one that wasn't submitted.

Heads up for honesty and they did change processes and speak to the AMHP. So, the initial call said they were not concerned with speaking to me after the call, the legally required report to admit me was never done. That left the outrageous in between interview, with the infamous two, though I would not learn about that for several months.

I have my suspicions as to why the report wasn't filed but as things come to light, I leave you to decide.

The next day would be a very interesting one. The locksmiths were brilliant, changing all other entry locks very quickly. The process of completing the car purchase took only 10 minutes, with electronic submission of change of ownership and the car gone.

I received a call stating that I would have to be ready for 12pm as that's when I would be taken. I should say this, when discussing such things, Mental Health Services never offer options. You are given a time and its made plain that is the time it is.

I responded saying I had a delivery from Amazon, I had to supply my MP and the CQC with additional information, as well as I had to pick up prescriptions from the pharmacy that related to my diabetes (I had been diagnosed about 3 weeks before).

I also had to follow up with the Police and several preparation things I had to get done.

Initially the Mental Health team refused to delay that long, so I said OK I will just let the various parties know you are denying me my rights to access the CQC and my local MP.

Reluctantly they then agreed an out of hours option to pick me up at 6pm and they agreed to wait at the bottom of the road, rather than draw attention with an ambulance outside my house.

In the rest of the time, I put additional clothes that my friend could pick up in case I was away for more than 7 days, I put a whole raft of things to one side to put out for my wife, that she could collect at the weekend.  I had fitted all the window locks and was ready to go.

One of the things about the mental health team is how unsubtle they are.  I understand if someone is very ill, they need people to know they are officials.

However, when coming round to a private house they parade their identification and without asking, before and after the conversations they had with me, would wander around outside the property. They could not get more attention from my neighbours if they sold tickets.

So, the ambulance turned up around 6pm. The AMHP was not happy about being called out of hours and to top it all, it turned out they had nowhere for me to go. So, after parking the ambulance the AMHP wandered up and down the road on the phone with his credentials swinging for 2-3 hours.

It turned out I was being taken to a mental health unit about 60 miles away.  The ambulanceman in the back of the unit with me was a great bloke.  We chatted all the way to the unit.

On the way he was telling me how mental health had changed and how it was much more drug orientated now.  As a youth he said that he had been engaged with Mental Health but at that time they spent a lot of time talking, rather than medicating.

We got to the mental health unit about 10pm. Well, it was a single room, with multiple cameras, with 2 staff on at all times, 24 hours a day, watching you from an attached room. Should be good for getting a cup of tea I thought, with such personal service. Actually, to be fair in that regard it was quite good.

The first thing that they did was take all my belongings. I was allowed to keep my phone thankfully, but they wouldn't let me take a pad and a pen from my bag because "it was night". I also wasn't allowed to change my clothes or shower for the same reason.

The room was the sort of space that you were more likely to bounce off something than hurt yourself, lots of ultra-soft furniture and beanbags.

I had also asked for a second pillow as the pillow I had was very thin and I cough at night unless my head is raised.  I didn't get that pillow until the 4th or 5th day.

I had put my faith in the fact that when I got to hospital, they would make their own independent assessments.  I didn't realise that there is an endemic approach, that assumes there is no smoke without fire and I noticed from my conversations how slanted the questions were and how what I would say would be selectively summarised as something very different.

I had a late-night conversation (about 11pm) with a medical doctor, something like a receiving examination to document how you are on arrival.

As with all of the doctors at the hospital, he asked about my book I had written, I offered to show him, he declined.  Many months later I would see that the doctor said I had delusions about writing the book.  This was a theme, two of the doctors also said my writing a book was delusional, despite me offering to show them the book (it was my previous book, maybe you read it…).

What I said and I said this to each doctor was quite simple.  I had written one book, I was researching 3 other books, in the very early stages.  Each I was trying to contact the key parties before deciding whether to move forward.

I said my aim was to write books about subjects that people wouldn't have read about but for which there was a lot of interest and my aim was to make these books accessible to understand just what achievements each were and just how incredible the journey was.

The subjects were the eradication of Polio as a disease, how Google Search came in to being and how the world switched from Aerials and Cables to Streaming in particular Netflix.

All are complicated by the nascent approach of not being able to contact senior execs electronically and the habit of a lot of technology companies about keeping key contacts hidden. It is understandable due to the sheer numbers of people that would otherwise be contacting those emails.

In the case of Polio, there are 6 key organisations to navigate. I explained that this was why I had multiple possibilities. Little did I know then my next book would actually be about what was happening at that moment.

What this doctor wrote (I have all the source documents as evidence) was that I had written a book in a couple of days and wrote 4 books to solve world problems. This was given as an example of my delusional state. Bear in mind I wouldn't see this for another 5 months!

What he also wrote (and I realised much later that there is a lot of cut and pasting going on so once it's in one document its all over the place) was that I had little insight into my current mental state.

This was the mania they were referring to that I wasn't actually experiencing.  Though I was unaware, what had been written at the time (but from my voice notes I was very wary about the doctor) this was a theme where anything that could be used to seem like it fitted a previous diagnosis was used.

What these people hadn't considered is I may actually have proof of these things.  More later.

They told me to get some sleep and I asked for them to turn the lights off.  They messed around and some peripheral lights were lowered but no luck with the main lights and no change, the lights were bright and despite several other requests stayed that way for the 2 days I was in the room.

The weird thing is they kept asking about me sleeping and I kept trying but I said I need you to turn the lights down a bit for me to sleep. I bundled all my clothes together to try to fashion a second pillow that would raise my head, stop my coughing and allow me to get some sleep.

They wouldn't allow me access to my things that night for a shower (because it was night) and told me I would have to wait to get access to my things, until I saw the doctor.  Later after not sleeping due to the lights and not having access to my things to wash and change, the doctor noted I seemed a bit dishevelled (from a report I saw much later).

The one advantage I had was having my phone and later I would realise this was a much better solution, as you can hear my state of mind, on my voice notes, which I could use in the event of a tribunal, complaints, a book etc. So, I took nearly 100 voice mails in the first several days and after every key conversation.

I had slept for 9 hours the previous day and so was not worried about only getting a few hours' sleep.

During the night because of the lights and second pillow, I had mentioned I was only getting cat naps, just the sort of necessity sleep. About 4am the nurses came in with medication for me to take. They wouldn't tell me what the medication was. This was the first of a number of times. I told them I was there for assessment, there was nothing wrong with me and I wouldn't take anything that could interfere with my faculties.

My 2 nurses changed from very friendly, to very unfriendly very quickly. They left the room; they wouldn't answer me for the rest of their shift (I found out this is common if you don't do what they say) and they turned all the lights up to absolute maximum. As a result I ended up without access to water or tea for several hours, despite repeated requests and there being 2 full time staff assigned to me.

The strange thing was I found this kind of funny. However, for anyone vulnerable it has overtones of nastier things.

During the night someone tried to fix the lighting. I was told there was a key that allowed the lights to be switched of but it had broken, inside the lock. Apparently other than that, they could only dim the lights a little.

Sometime in the night my legs had become inflamed and very itchy. I had only been diagnosed with diabetes a few weeks before and it was possible that it was related to my prescription, or possibly related to the diabetes itself. I had told the doctor late the previous night but I could see that they may become a problem, if untreated.

DO WHAT I SAY
DO WHAT I SAY

# Chapter 9

I had a fairly sleepless night with cat naps.  The psychiatrist doctor noted by the way I had trouble sleeping.  It should be noted that bipolar is often triggered by lack of sleep.

When I met the junior doctor, in the morning the next day (who would be involved throughout), I asked whether I could record the conversations and she refused to allow it.  I was concerned as it had become obvious, the conversations were not open but slanted, so I wanted to document this. I had been very open to being assessed, as long as it was a real assessment.

When talking generally the doctor would intersperse with "so you are having racing thoughts" when I explained I enjoyed writing or "so you are taking on too much" when I explained my next projects, when I had said nothing of the sort and I corrected that.  Knowing that these phrases can be associated with conditions and these phrases were being forced from innocent phrases, I became wary.

The doctor then asked to be able to consult with my next of kin. Whatever my wife had said to the mental health team had been enough for them to decide to engage with me.  I knew that this could only be bad for me.

It was clear that whatever my wife had said, that they could use as evidence, would allow them to tip the scales. I could tell by just how keen the doctor was to get this agreement and she wouldn't take no for an answer, though it was clear I had to say yes. I was not going to allow them to substitute what they could see, with the situation seen through the eyes of my wife who was still clearly affected by 2015. I closed that door so hard on that idea that it would rattle, although the doctor persisted.

Weeks later I would read that she also wrote that I had delusions of writing a book. This is despite the fact that I offered to show her the book and she waved that away (if you don't see it, even though it's in his bag, maybe it doesn't exist. Like a perverse Schrodinger's cat argument).

Interestingly all the junior doctors "forget" to mention that I had sent copies of this book to my MP and the Mental Health Services Minister and the CQC i.e., that there was proof which I had mentioned.

I told this doctor, as I told each of them that because we were relatively frugal with me not working, I was only seeking a publishing deal which did not involve me paying, i.e. either a traditional publishing deal or I would use Amazon.

What the doctor wrote was "I had been seeking financial support from friends and family". Again, this supports the idea of mania where spending gets out of control. I had specifically stated the opposite.

She also wrote that I believed my car had been stolen when it was on my drive. I had sold my car, written a review on google reviews about it with correspondence and quotes on the day in question. It much later became clear this was copied from the infamous two report that my admission relied upon.

There is much more. I raised a complaint about this document with the trust some 12 months ago, analysing every line in the document as almost every line was not true. It is still being worked on, apparently.

However, a number of the claims were those raised by the infamous two. They had said I wasn't sleeping. What I told them was I was sleeping really well, except for the day my wife left me.

I asked the doctor for a copy of the admissions report at the end of the discussion. When I had said I wanted to record the conversation before we started, she had said no it's not necessary you can just get a copy of the report at any time.

After the conversation had finished, when I asked her how could I get a copy of the report, she said speak to IT and refused further questions. No one else knew what that meant.

Several days later they submitted the report to my GP, not realising I was checking my patient record every day for updates.

Later the junior doctor came back and said that they would want to prescribe abilify.  I made clear that I would not take abilify under any circumstances.  The junior doctor said that they could section me and then they would be able to forcibly medicate me.

I said that I would take sectioning rather than abilify but I wanted an immediate tribunal as I wanted to present my evidence

Shortly after in one of only a few times I met the consultant of the unit. The consultant came in and said that in watching me 24/7 they could find nothing wrong with me but he wanted a longer period to assure themselves, with me in the general population in the facility.

This was the last time that prescribing me anti-psychotics was discussed. I have to say the person with the most moderate pragmatic approach and the person with whom I could have the most sensible conversations was the consultant in charge.

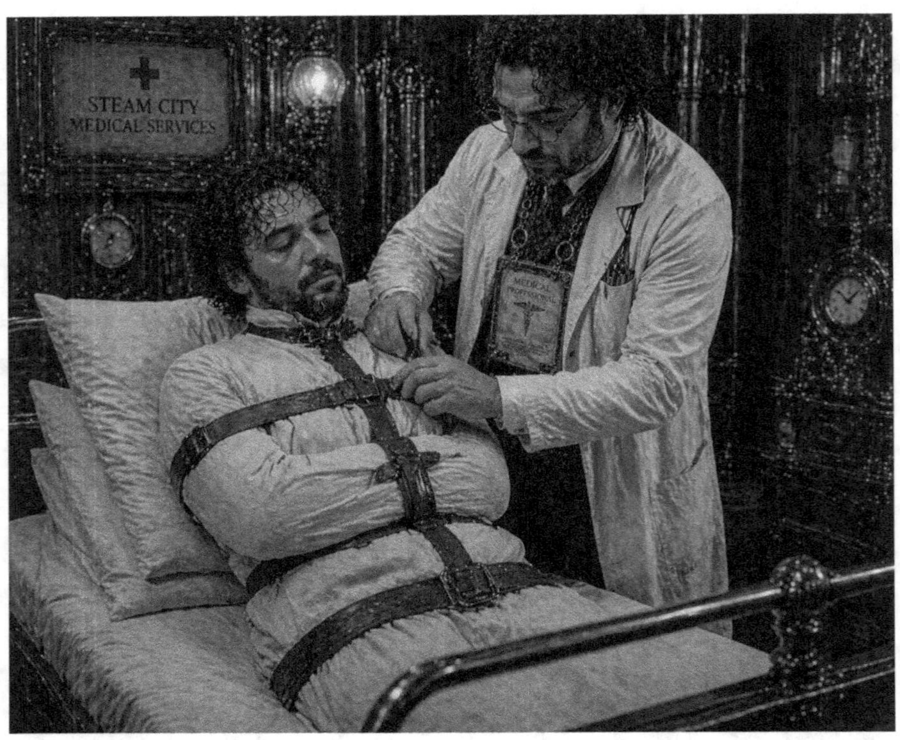

I had been expecting that they would want to keep me in a ward to monitor me and was keen for this to happen as up until now all I could write about was what had happened to me, alone in an isolation room. I was actually looking forward to this in a number of ways.

I could get to spend time with people and see their conditions clearly, not through my own illness like I experienced in 2015. I could get to know them as people, I could see how they were dealt with and treated.

# Chapter 10

I was transferred onto the main ward. This was the first time I realised I was not actually on a mental health assessment unit but a long-term ward. I will move onto all the people I met but before I do we have to deal with MelonBallGate.

When I first went into the Mental Health Unit, I ended up sleeping in t-shirt and jeans because I was being monitored by 2 people constantly. In the first few days of being on the ward I did the same as I has been on high frequency observations (standard when transferring from isolation). High frequency observations means that they were looking in on me something like every 15-30 minutes.

Apologise for the details in what follows here but will keep it to just the key things needed to understand what was happening.

I woke up at around 4am my jeans were very uncomfortable and I could tell that there was substantial swelling. When I looked, my left testicle was the size of a small melon. I was freaked out, as you can imagine. In the same way if you saw a melon size growth by your eye or something. I contacted the night staff by going to their "staff room" to say I needed to be seen by A&E urgently.

#

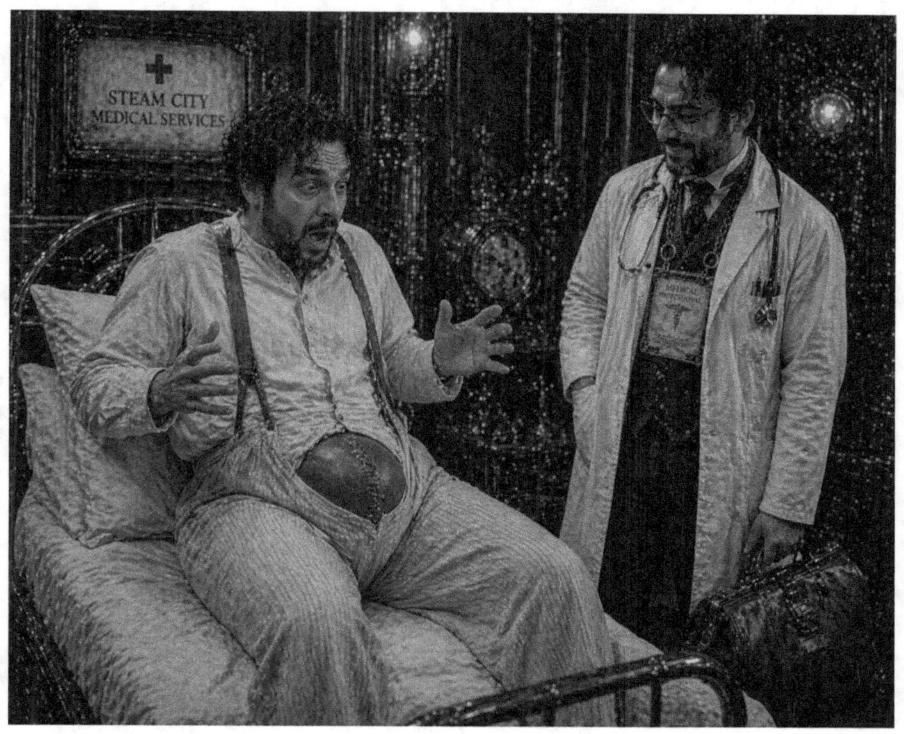


On the main ward were all the different individual rooms for patients and on the main corridor all the communal areas and toilets. Until I was actually placed on the ward, I didn't realise that the only difference between voluntary patients and sectioned patients were whether you could open your own door to your room or not.

This was very light handed in relation to sectioning where in other locations it could be much scarier.

In the middle of the main corridor was a locked glass enclosed room, where the staff would go to work on their paperwork etc.  At night it was not uncommon to see all the staff in the room for extended periods.

Some shifts were worse than others but, on some of those night shifts it was like no one wanted to deal with a patient.  When that happens you often see queues build up outside the room, where people are waiting to be seen. The staff sometimes will ignore people for as long as they could before answering, I think to discourage them from doing it.

I knocked urgently explained the situation and one of the senior staff said I would first have to be examined by the staff on duty and they would then decide what should happen next.  I showed two people the issue and I was told that a doctor would be called.  This would have been about 4:15 ish maybe (I have voice records covering this whole time).

Every ½ hour or so I would go and ask what was happening and I was told, the doctor was informed and would be there when he got there.

By the time it had gone past half past six I decided I had to do something as it seemed clear no doctor had actually been called in the previous 2 ¼ hours.

One of the things I had come to realise is that as a patient proving something is actually quite difficult.  For the hospital, the more records they keep the more they can point to evidence.  However, what does the patient have.  For me I had started copying people and organisations that couldn't be refuted by the trust, the more I realised the situation.

In this case, I called 111 and went through my issues with them. I knew that there would be both a written assessment that was dated and timed and also the recorded call/transcript.

I was assessed and told I must go to A&E within the hour.  I explained that I was next to the hospital but couldn't go because I was in a mental health unit and they wouldn't let me go.

The 111-assessor asked to speak to people on shift and told them I needed to go to A&E and it needed to be within the hour.  They said that the doctor was on his way and would assess.

Shortly after I was told the doctor was enroute by a very pissed off nurse on the ward.  The doctor arrived about ½ hour later and decided that I should go to radiology rather than A&E for a scan. That was booked for about 10am.

I was accompanied to the scan.  Afterwards, I asked every couple of hours as to what was happening and I was told it was waiting on doctors' recommendations.

Months later I found out that the radiologist's report had been sent back early afternoon, yet it was another 22 hours before I was allowed to go to A&E.  The radiologists report highlighted a possible differential diagnosis of infarction on the right testicle caused by the swelling of the left which was an urgent matter.

When I was finally allowed to go to A&E, I was accompanied to the A&E and then left there on my own (this was about 100 metres away from where I was staying).  The doctor in the mental health unit had not marked the case as urgent, despite this now being 32 hours after I had reported it.

When I was seen by an A&E doctor and then a consultant about 4 hours later (they were brilliant by the way but were not told it was urgent), I was told I had possible torsion (where the blood supply is cut off) on the right testicle and it may have died due to my failure to go to A&E immediately.

Subsequently it emerged that although blood supply had been constricted this was not in fact torsion but an urgent operation was scheduled for 2 weeks later on both testicles.

I raised a formal complaint with the Mental Health Trust responsible for the Mental Health Ward with the information I knew at the time. Without my agreement and against their complaints procedure the trust converted this to a so called Rapid Response, which just looks at what the documentation says has happened (so no real investigation).

I eventually got hold of the response which stated that I never alerted the staff to the condition, instead they raised the concern with the doctor.

Only one problem I saw for that. My 111 call which was recorded by the NHS and on which the night staff actually spoke to 111. When I realised this, I requested GDPR for every interaction I had with every organisation from the day the Crisis team first contacted me. It took a lot of time and effort but it was worth it.

And the records for the Trust, no mention of our many interactions at all and a record showing me seeing the doctor while I was actually on the phone to 111 and before the doctor had actually been called. I had the transcript and the voice call and the staff member on the call giving the update.

This complaint was converted back to a formal complaint and is still being investigated 1 year later.

I also have multiple voice notes I had taken around this whole event. This mean that records appear to have been fraudulently updated and the Trust was using those as the basis of its "truth" as to what had happened.

During this time my leg which had been itchy red and so dry it was turning to flakes was getting worse and I saw the start of infection.  It was 3 days since I had told doctors I needed medication and shown them the prescription script.  It would be nearly 6 days in total before I would see that medication and in the interim the leg became quite badly infected.

3 days later I developed an infection related to my major swelling, I was told I had to wait for someone to accompany me to A&E.  After 6 hours of waiting, I was told I was informal so could have gone on my own, it was just no one told me that.  Due to the delay of getting to A&E, by the time I was seen by A&E I couldn't get the medication ordered that day and it was 36 hours before I received it.

The above are just examples for what happened to me in the mental health ward.  In talking to the patients on the ward they were fairly typical of the way that the staff dealt with medical issues.  One of the patients explained it to me thus: "This is one place you don't want to get ill."

# Chapter 11

Now to life on the ward. The ward that I was on was male. Additionally, the majority of the patients were fundamentally really good people who had just hit a tough spot.

This was very different to the wards I had been on in 2015 where people, like me at the time, were severely ill and to be honest, some of them were pretty scary, while in a vulnerable state.

There were no fights or major altercations in the time I was there. There were raised voices but generally those were pleas for help from people, after they found themselves ignored over a period of time.

Overall, a thoroughly friendly bunch in the main with some incredible stories. I was the only person on the ward that wasn't medicated and it opened my eyes as to the impact of these drugs on people.

People used to literally walk up and down the corridors aimlessly and that probably is a vision people have about such wards. The reality is because they have so little to captivate their interests.

I spent the best part of nine days talking to people and it was kind of funny, wherever I went after a while, I would get a little queue of people who wanted to talk to me. It was actually quite sweet. I will say I did stand out there, from everyone else I met, they were unfortunately quite ill.

What I suppose I hadn't always considered is that whilst a few of the patients, engaged widely in discussions and were both entertaining and engaging a lot seemed very reticent with other patients, maybe because they knew that they also were ill and because of the effect of the medication on their thinking.

However, it was still sad to see the light snuffed out of their eyes, their brains too clogged to think or process from the medication. I wondered many times whether the sacrifice of the person was always worth it and whether there was another way.

So, my conversations took time, people needed time to think and what I saw very quickly is they almost all were craving that interaction. It was really nice to see a number of patients really come out of their shell, over the time that I was there.

The ward I was on had really nice rooms (for mental health wards). Which were very simply but recently decorated, extremely clean with plenty of individual space, even a bit of space to walk around in. There were plenty of showers and toilets, the ward was always kept extremely clean.

There was a large TV in one of the rooms with enough seating space for a dozen people and another smaller meeting room where people played chess. Tea and Coffee which were both decaffeinated, were available 24/7, though in the evenings/night you would almost always have to brave the Goldfish room that the employees sat in to get cups and milk.

The food was good, nutritious, the staff friendly that served it. It was always served on time and after lunch and dinner, the area became a games area for about an hour or so.

Staff would join in on the games and some staff really put the effort to mix and teach patients. Maybe 6 times a day there was a call for vapes and everyone that vaped plus those who wanted a gasp of fresh air could get 10 minutes outside.

The ward was always organised and they always dispensed medications on time and took various tests at set times. It was all very organised and with many of the patient's long term, they all knew where they should be.

Fundamentally the place was well maintained and well run regards the basics of keeping you washed, medicated and fed. Let me introduce you to some of the people on the ward.

# Chapter 12

There was a lovely guy on the ward with a life changing condition. Since he was a teenager his memories only lasted (from what he told me and what I saw) between 15 minutes and an hour and rarely up at that top end.

He carried around with him a pile of sticky notes, which he had amassed over time with hints, tips and directions. However, he couldn't tell which were important and he ran out of time when he was reviewing them.

All he wanted to do was to get out and go home to his family.

We spoke every day; many times and it was sad to see each time he looked at you, the lack of recognition in his eyes. Instead, what you saw was a confusion, as to whether he already knew you and was expected to recognise you.

I was amazed how well he dealt with it, though obviously sometimes the frustration of it all won out. More than anything the sticky notes, almost added to the confusion as he didn't know where to focus.

I spent time with him every day, which he obviously didn't remember. I gave him a pad and tried to work with him to just put a title and some bullet points he would know, that they were the most important. It reminded me of memento and those crucial post-it clues as to what needed to be done next.

Unfortunately, he didn't want me touching the pad, when I gave it to him, so I couldn't write the things he always bought up. I think he didn't want someone else's writing he didn't recognise and wanted to do it himself, so he knew when he later looked at the notes, that he could trust them.

Next time I saw him I asked about the pad, he said he had a blank pad but didn't know how or why. To really help this guy all he needed long term is someone to help him manage this as best he can.

I have to say though it's an inspiration to the human spirit that with all that to contend with, we managed to laugh together many times. He may not remember but I will for him.

There was a young guy on the ward that was obviously extremely intelligent but also very timid. If I had to choose a character from the movies, he reminded me of, it was Bambi.

He was extremely aware of where everyone was and if anyone moved too fast or raised their voice in an unexpected way, he would disappear.

However, when you sat down and spent time with the guy, he was extremely clever but just incredibly wary. We developed quite a close friendship and spent many hours talking.

It was clear he was extremely well educated and he was a lovely guy. I have no idea whether something had happened to him or whether it was a long-held condition.

However, when I started asking about what he loved in life, it was music and I asked whether there was anything he knew more about than  anyone else, he spent hours talking to me about pickups on guitars and I was suddenly in a room with the most confident person in the room, where I had no doubt, he knew more about this subject than almost anyone else on the planet.

He explained the intricacies of how it worked, he had ideas for an invention based on proven technology that could change the market. He knew so much and became so confident you could just see, that people could mentor and bring out the absolute best in this guy.

There were no doubts that he had some serious problems but also after 30 years of mentoring as part of my role, the guy had huge potential and already had the ideas for how to make his mark on the world.

I hadn't played chess since I was 10 but spent at least an hour every day playing chess with him.  I noticed that while playing chess he had more confidence when talking.  Maybe because while playing he wasn't so self-aware.

Towards the end of my stay, his family visited each day. I am routing for him.  He was one of the really good guys.

I had mentioned that people milled around the corridors a lot.  I noticed after a day or so chatting to people, that people started to collect around me a little.

Sometimes a little wary, they wouldn't necessarily say anything, just be in the vicinity and when I was having conversations with others that were not private would often just hang around the area. After a while I deduced that some people got comfort from being near these conversations, even if they didn't have the confidence initially to partake in them.

There was a guy there who would have been say mid-fifties. He had been very senior in Mental Health services before becoming one of their patients.

Many people including this guy told me that this was common, especially amongst those who put the most into it. This guy had a very impressive career and was sought after within Mental Health Services.

One of the things I have noticed generally on the wards. People's confidence had been broken; you could literally feel their vulnerability. However, he was a lovely fellow and had many stories.

The impact of the medication on him was quite painful to watch. When he had to think, you would see him take a time out and come back sometimes 30 minutes later, with the answer. While he was there, you could almost feel him searching for an answer.

He had hit tough times which he stated up front. However, robbing him of the ability to think, also took his confidence. In moments of lucidity, it was clear he used to have a good mind. However, I loved spending time with him. He was such an empathetic person who had cared so much when working.

As with many of the others, the opportunity to spend time talking with someone showing interest in him would do wonders.

One of the real characters on the ward was about 30. He had suffered fairly serious mental health problems, which were sporadic and he didn't know why they had occurred though they appeared worse when drinking.

He had been hit by a truck, whilst having an episode (he didn't say whether he had walked into traffic, I am not sure if he knew). When he was hit, he had been thrown in the air and landed on his head doing some fairly serious damage to his skull.  In the ensuing accident one of his legs had suffered serious damage looking like some kind of animal had mauled him.

This guy was always smiling, always pleasant. He had been placed in mental health services because of his episodes but obviously, after such a serious crash he really needed specialist support.

Where the damage to his legs had severely affected that leg's muscles, tendons etc he had to develop a way of walking to get by with the leg.  His gait was severely impacted.  He never complained but when talking I asked about his physiotherapy to cope with the damage to his leg.  He had never been given any.

He had been waiting for many months as well, for them to arrange an MRI to see what the impact of the injury, was on his brain but apparently this was only just being done.

There were many such characters on the ward. Many were there for years rather than months.  A lot of nice people.  The most obvious thing missing was someone they could talk to.

Ultimately, from what I saw no one on the day to day ward staff had patient mental well being on their agenda.  Quite Ironic really.

There were patients worrying about housing and benefits for example when they got out.

The lack of any outlet to talk about these sorts of things eventually caused some screaming and shouting for help.  Instead of dealing with that the patient was transferred.

# Chapter 13

I saw from my patient record at my GP that the mental health ward had requested my patient records, apparently with my permission.

You guessed it, what permission. I raised a complaint with the CQC that fundamental rights such as GDPR were being ignored. On the 6th day I was there, suddenly I was presented with a document that asked amongst other things whether I would give my rights to my records being accessed to which I declined.

The nurse's face was a picture as they already had possession of my records for about 4 days.

This document I was given just told me about basic rights, which normally I believe you see on admission. Someone sat with me and asked me to sign each section while they waited.

They then took the document from me, never gave me a copy, despite requests. Next time I saw it, several Months later as part of a GDPR request.

At this point I would like to note, this was the only document I was given, in my time on the mental health wards. I saw through GDPR rafts of documents, I was apparently meant to sign (45 pages of 72-hour care plans, of which I was never shown any) left unsigned and never shown to me, during my time there, despite being updated every 72 hours.

I would never have signed these care plans as they contained many of the falsehoods I have previously mentioned and I would have raised that. Many of the points in conversations with the doctors I explicitly told them the opposite, but these comments were never documented. If I was being cynical, I would hazard a guess that is maybe why I was never given them.

As mentioned, I was never given a copy of the admissions summary, despite me asking. I was just fortunate that they sent it to my GP.

I have just found in my packs (I have thousands of pages of documents from my various GDPR requests), copies of ward reviews. Where these are different to other documents is that they have a dedicated note taker, they involve the full range of doctors and senior staff (i.e., witnesses) but also the Consultant in charge of the ward.

Many documents are prepared based on a doctor's recollection and chosen interpretation of events; the ward reviews record what was said.

Suddenly I am seeing statements that reflect what I actually said and the doctors who made the false statements, they were in these meetings too. Well, that could be awkward for some.

After 9 days a final Ward Review was held. The consultant said I was only suffering from physical health issues and it was time for me to leave. Note that at no time, during my 11 day stay did they actually find anything wrong with me, other than physical health issues. In fact their records are full of observations saying the opposite.

I said that given everything that had happened at the hospital and only recently getting my anti-biotic medication, I would like to stay a few more days in case of complications with the hospital, which was agreed.

# Chapter 14

After I got home, I raised a complaint on my physical experience re the upcoming operation and a complaint on the admissions document.

Now at this stage I had only seen the admissions document. For some background. I had been in senior management for 25 years at this point and in critical strategic positions in consultancies for 15 years.

I was used to constantly writing documents, whether sales, operational, development, strategic etc and reviewing many times that number. I had learnt that accuracy was critical at an extremely early stage in my career.

In my life I had never seen such an inaccurate document and I was staggered that such a document could exist unchecked. What was worse for me is that this is was a key document distributed to for example to my GP.

Originally, I submitted a simple complaint on the admissions document to the Trust, looking at the first several sentences and explaining how they were inaccurate. I explained that the rest of the document was the same and I had evidence to show this.

I imagined I would be contacted regarding the evidence (how else would they get it). About 4 months later, I questioned what had happened to both complaints. On the admissions document I was told they were nearly ready to respond.

Now how could they do that if I had the evidence, they knew that and did not contact me. That's like investigating a murder without interviewing the witnesses.

Anyway, on the admissions document, I spelt out every instance where the document was wrong and submitted evidence for the same (I have even evidence more now). It was 8,000 words and 29 A4 pages (it was honestly that bad).

Some examples of just how bad the admissions document was throughout, the admissions document stated: -

- **I was seen by the Crisis team following concerns raised by a family friend.** From the actual notes of the call referred to (there was only one) said my friend "did not see or have concerns"
- **He is claiming to have written a book.** I offered to show her the book (I had the book with me), I had sent a copy to my MP and had a reply, Mind had sent me an email re their use of the book which I had a copy of. I told the doctor this.
- **Appears fixated that they are going to flee to Japan.** I wasn't. The crisis team just doorstepped me whilst 999 was following up on an all-ports alert and interfered in my responding to them over several calls (which was the entirety of my meeting with the Crisis Team).

  An extract from the ward review (a meeting a bit later, with the Consultant of the ward and with the author of this Admissions Document present) "he realised his wife had taken passports and he was concerned that they would leave the country." Concerned not Fixated. It was valid hence the Police issued an All-Ports Alert.

- **He has made several calls to police to warn them he believes they will try to leave the country.**  I was concerned see above, I called them (999).  They then called me 6 times (I have the police logs).  The Crisis team (the infamous duo) knew this as they were there for the calls and knew why they called.  The police were running checks such as movement of funds in joint bank accounts, whether any of my things had been taken, recent pictures of my wife and daughter, passport numbers and copies of passports etc).  Later this was deliberately misrepresented and cut and pasted by the doctors without even saying that this was just what a third party had said.

- **he has written a book...   ...regarding global issues in particular polio eradication and has been seeking financial support from friends and family to support this.**  I said it was about my recovery (it's the first book I wrote, which I had with me... like I wouldn't know the subject).  From the ward review it said that I had written a book "which explains his struggles as a mental health patient."  In regards financial support I said the opposite, that I couldn't afford to self-publish and could only accept a traditional publishing model or Amazon model.  I have emails to show this is exactly what I discussed

- **and believes his car had been stolen despite it being on the drive.**  I later found out this was a cut and paste from the meeting with the infamous duo.
  I had moved the car onto the drive (my friend was there), I had sold the car the day after (I had quotes for the car before and after my meeting with the infamous duo) and it was picked up and a google review left the morning after that, which was the morning of my admission.  I had a lot of evidence on this and this was just plain invention.

- **Speech: Pressure of speech – Tangential. Difficult to interrupt. Moderate tone**
  I have circa 80 voice recordings surrounding all events including this meeting. I was wary of this doctor, meaning I was very aware of what I said. From ward review (less than 1 hour after) "His speech was fast but not pressured, he could be interrupted"
- **Mood: Objectively and subjectively euthymic.** Euthymic is a word with bipolar connotations even though it means calm and steady state.
- **Flight of ideas. Grandiose delusions – has written 4 books to solve global issues. Wrote an entire book in the space of a couple of days.** This is not even consistent with earlier message. I have outlined before. From ward review "on his way to write another book, has thought about various topics, like global eradication of polio. He has written to WHO, UNICEF, CDC, Bill Gates and the Rotary Club" and "He has also emailed Google Executive and Netflix". These were the other 3 books.

This gives you a small insight but the whole document was the same. This is what they sent to my doctor. As of the time of writing this complaint has been worked on for nearly 12 months. No one has contacted me at all ever, to talk to me about this.

So far on the complaints I have raised, no one has contacted me at all from the investigating teams for anything. My complaints cover now over 250 A4 pages of failings with evidence, with over 100 pages over 6 months old and yet no one has contacted me.

I won't go through the other complaints in full just give a few examples -

- I was put in an assessment unit without the legally required paperwork needed to do so (the assessment by doctors that I needed to go to the unit).  This paperwork was never filed.  I do not see this as a coincidence and potentially makes taking me for assessment illegal..
- Because I was let out too early in 2015 and had to be readmitted shortly after release, this classification treated the incident as reoccurring rather than a one off life event.
- This meant that all anyone was interested in, was putting me back on abilify and it was made clear at every stage the only basis on which I would not be taken away would be if I started taking the drug. It was used like blackmail.  Do this or you go away.
- I was threatened with sectioning by a junior doctor to forcibly administrate anti-psychotics, despite them not being able to find anything wrong with me.  A fact confirmed less than 1 hour later by the consultant.
- The notes on my 2 hours phone call from the Crisis Team showed no concerns yet I was pursued the following day.
- The crisis team meeting was deliberately carried out whilst I was being called on the emergency police line (999) by police regarding an all-ports alert. The team sat through several calls from the police, interrupted my attempts to assist the police and deal with the requests made by the police trying to establish circumstances. In America that is an arrestable offence.

- One of the crisis team wrote a request for a mental health act Assessor and made outrageous claims, for example that I believed my car was stolen despite it being on my drive. I have lots of proof that I had no such belief (as discussed before), however he forgot to tell his colleague about the wild claims. They wrote a second request but to a different department with none of the wild claims in it.
- The mental health trust did not even attempt to follow their own complaints procedures. In 12 months I have not heard who is investigating my complaints, how long they will take to investigate, when it will complete.
- The Mental Health Trust haven't asked me a single question on my hundreds of pages of evidence backed complaints, they haven't asked me what I am looking for from the complaints. All of the above they are meant to ask immediately on the complaint being raised.
- The complaints don't even mention when they go past the mandatory period they are allowed to take to respond by the NHS.
- The Trust has taken up to 8 weeks to send an acknowledgement letter of receipt of the complaint rather than the 3 days they are meant to.

# Chapter 15

Have you ever tried talking to a brick wall? Ah many of you will say yes. Ok a follow up question. Have you ever successfully talked to a brick wall?

That's more like it. So going back to when my wife left, all means of communicating with her stopped working suddenly.

As I have outlined, I sent many messages after my wife left, going through the whole gamut of possibilities and emotions. I literally didn't know what was happening. I realised after a short while, my wife wasn't going to communicate with me at all.

At one point in the first evening, I realised that my wife still had the car but I was the named driver on the insurance, I still owned the vehicle etc. So, I had said please don't use the car, without talking to me on WhatsApp. If I didn't hear, I wrote I would cancel the insurance and road tax.

Whilst this may look heavy handed, my wife had written off two cars a few months before and I was unsure of her state. Also, this was designed to try to get a conversation going, so we could at least talk and I could know what was going on. Instead, the car was dumped on the road and the key posted through the letterbox.

The one thing I learnt was the fact that my wife, though invisible on WhatsApp, was still reading the messages 3-4 hours after. From this point onwards, all my energy had been directed towards using WhatsApp to communicate. Before this I didn't know if she had switched phones or numbers, or whether she would see anything I wrote.

I realised after that; my wife was reading my messages, though not responding to any of them and this gave me a channel to update my wife.  As such if I had letters for her, or needed to update her on anything, or to ask for messages to be passed to my daughter (before my daughter started messaging me), I had a channel to do so.

Also, for example, if I was going to request info, from the school on my daughter's progress, I let my wife know so we didn't have an issue etc.  In 12 months, my wife has never responded to me but continues to monitor the WhatsApp.  I also used it to let her know what items I was putting out for her to collect etc.

Sometimes talking to a brick wall is all you have.

# Chapter 16

I spent about 3 months of this year painting.  I mean painting walls, windows, doors, shed's.  Talking to my brother about this we spent time discussing how therapeutic this is.  I have never painted before.

I used to watch painters and decorators, coming in to the pub with paint spattered from head to toe and I thought, if this is what it looks like when professionals do it, I can imagine the devastation I would cause.

Honestly, although I now feel a bit stupid about that, I just imagined paint to be an incredibly difficult substance to manage, that would end up all over me and all the surfaces I didn't want to touch.

What did I know.  Anyway, we have lived in the property we are in for 17 years.  It is a rented property and I might have mentioned in my previous book we have had a very good relationship with the landlord and his mother.

They are really good people and from the start, we only asked for anything, if it really needed to be done and if we could do it ourselves, we would.

On their part as the years passed by, they continually went above and beyond what they needed to do, showing a trust and a wish for us to treat the house as our home.  Even when we had to change locks over time, they didn't ask for a copy and if they needed access at all, dealt with us in a way as though it was our home.

It has been a relationship of incredible respect and I am thankful to have been part of it.

We have always been told to decorate as we wanted to.  I decided when my wife left that since we had been here so long and it hadn't been decorated since, that I would deal with some of the painting in the rooms that needed it most.

We have a fantastic jack of all trades that we know and he painted the bathroom for us and did a great job. He had some paint left over and I decided I would just use that up.

I painted a door on a container unit and applied 3 coats of the relevant paint. It was at this point I found out about primer (I didn't know). After a few days, several areas had broken up and I sanded back to base, spent some time on the internet and bought some primer, as I should have done at the start. I was surprised I didn't get paint anywhere I didn't want and none on my clothes.

I decided to paint a few more doors, so proceeded to paint inside and outside, of all the doors on the property. I then started on window frames, that given the years had suffered from exposure to the elements. I found the intricacies of so many surfaces, really calming almost like meditating. I ended up painting window frames, inside and out.

I realise now that this can become addictive, as I moved onto first outside walls, a large shed and then painting all the rooms (but one) inside the house. By the end, I just wore my normal clothes as I just didn't have the problems I foresaw, with paint splatter.

I now wonder whether the professionals have shops, that sell paint splattered clothes to put prospective painters like me off painting

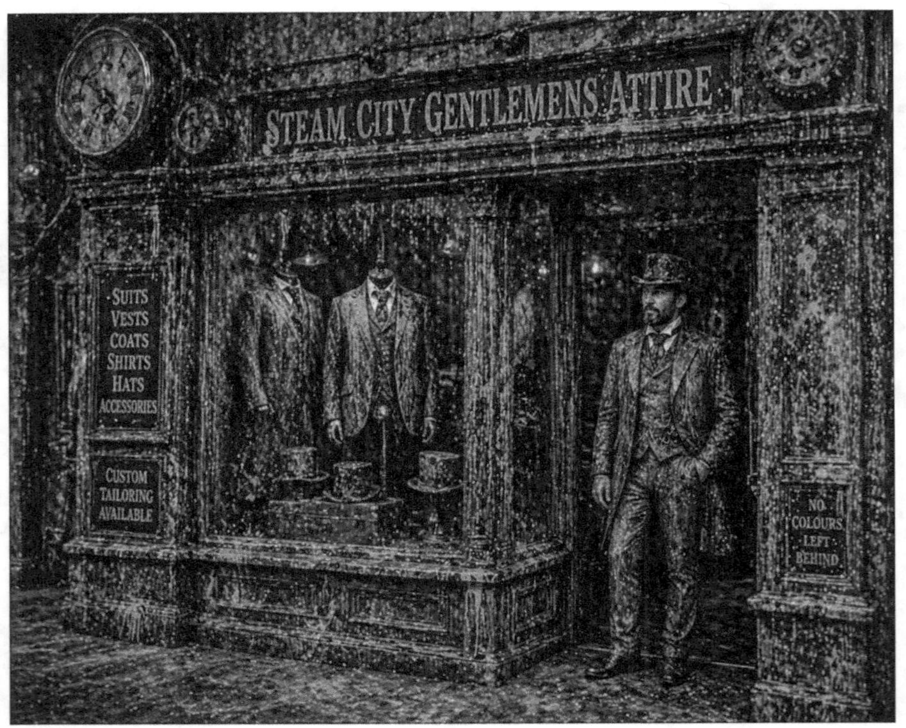


I never thought about this at the time but I think maybe part of the reason, I spent so long painting is that I found it such a therapeutic thing to do, after my wife had moved out, it calmed my soul a little.

# Chapter 17

In relation to my wife, it's quite difficult.   Without knowing what happened, you never really know where you stand.  You never get to put your side, or understand what you could have changed.

I have become accustomed to not knowing.  In some ways, I have become used to it, dealt with it and built a reality around what I can.

Through the year I have gradually worked through the house and worked out what I believed my wife would want, that she hadn't taken.  It has taken some time.

I hadn't realised that my wife was a bit of a hoarder.  Actually, that is an understatement.  My wife never threw anything away, not a single thing related to my daughter; it appears ever.  I wondered why our house seemed gradually, to fill up with things everywhere. When I started emptying cupboards, to work out what my wife would want, I began to see.

For example, take Looms.  These are small elastic bands you knit on a small frame to form bracelets etc.  My daughter was enamoured by Looms for I am guessing a month or two.  This was maybe about 10 years ago.  I just kept finding bags of unopened looms.  I think it probably totalled 30 to 50,000 bands.

It just made the process of going through these things, so much more difficult.  In the end we got into a ritual, where I would leave out items in a secured area, my wife would collect over the next couple of months.  Anything she didn't want, some I would store; some I would throw (I had to reduce the sheer clutter).

The whole not talking thing makes it interesting as I have no idea of how much space my wife has, or needs so you spend time putting things out to see if they are taken and then put more of that type if so.   What I have done is clear out the storage of other items (what was in there) and started leaving items longer term in storage areas, so my wife can take her time to decide whether she wants it.

The only time my wife has communicated with me at all, was to ask for permission for my daughter to go on a trip abroad with her to get away from all the pressures from her school work and the disruption in her life.  With some guarantees I obviously gave it.

This was very decent of my wife, she could have taken my daughter, without telling me but she did.  This is an important step in at least building trust between us.

I have written some things to her, to try to allow us to have some capacity to interact but I have no idea whether she reads them.  Our daughter is at that age, that she will be 18 in 18 months' time and it's important I allow her to interact, with me, at a pace she is comfortable with.

Ultimately, I want my wife to be OK and her being OK, is critical to my daughter as well.  Ultimately the situation is what it is and I have decided, that I cannot let someone else change who I am.  I don't want to carry hurt or any residual upset.  Also, I want my wife to be happy, with whatever that means, to her.  It really is a case of if you love someone enough, then let them go.

It is also the only way, I will ever be able to move on.

# Chapter 18

Building a relationship back with my daughter is obviously extremely important to me. In many of her formative years I was there but not actually there.

As you will see from my last book, since I had been gone cognitively for so long, she hadn't seen the me I was, from before, since the age of 8. I like to believe I was a loving dad and never really got over the fact that we had made such a lovely daughter.

Every weekend was a family weekend. We every now and again had family over but most weekends were just us and my memories are just full of love and laughter in that period. I took many tens of thousands of pictures of us during those 8 years.

In terms of connection, one of my friends said to me that women connect immediately with babies in the womb but for men, it's when you first see them and particularly the first time, they touch your hand or you touch their cheek, that it suddenly and overwhelmingly hits. That was the case for me. From the moment she touched my hand I was devoted.

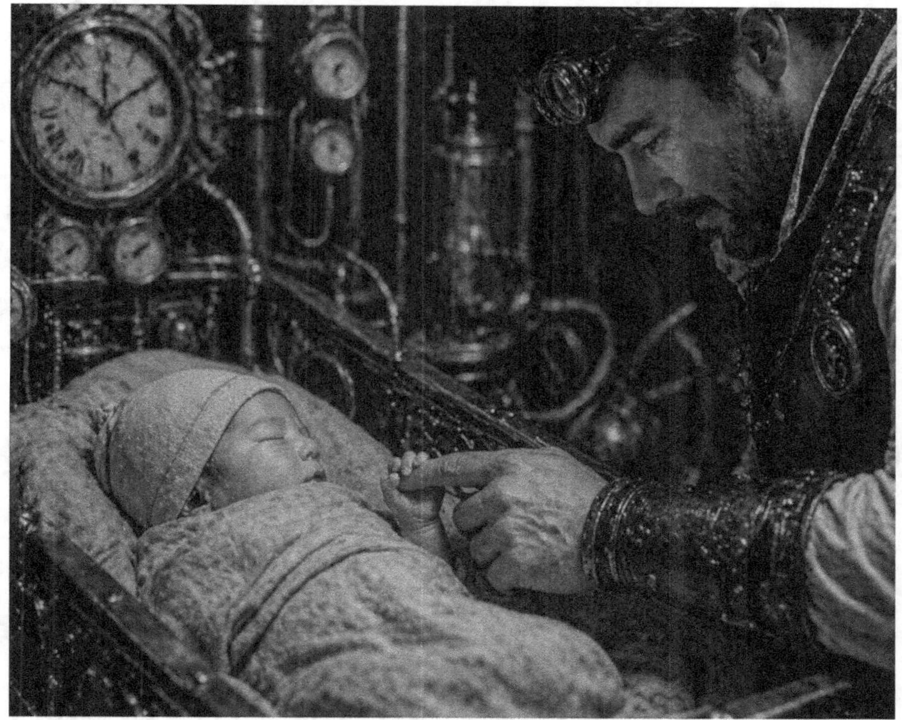

That's not to say, I didn't enjoy the pregnancy period; we were so happy about having a baby. When my wife and daughter left, initially things were coordinated between them, like going invisible on WhatsApp, at exactly the same time.

I made some longer-term decisions, quite soon upfront. My dad and my mum split up, when I was 11 after many years of them arguing at night, almost every night. My dad after, wouldn't really talk about my mother at all and carried a silent anger towards her in his veins through his life, though he never said a bad word about her.

My mum poisoned me and my younger sister against my dad, on an ongoing and semi-permanent basis and there was such open nastiness and vindictiveness about it, I never forgot it.  My mum made my older brother and sister leave home when they turned 16 and with me threw me out as soon as the child benefit stopped (that week).

This was about 6 weeks before my A levels and with virtually no notice.  Luckily my dad found somewhere for me to stay.  For the next 6 weeks leading up to my exams, I ate twice a week when I went round my dads to see him.

The reason I say this, is just seeing first hand how poisonous this can become and how that pain can be carried so tightly for life, I was determined it wouldn't be like that.

The initial reactions on both sides did escalate, when I was scrambling to understand what was going on and with everything that happened with mental health involvement and the landlord contact, I initially thought it was malicious.

It was clear because of how close my daughter was with my wife and that they spent so much time together that the first thing I needed to do was give them space, to heal from whatever was causing them pain.  So, I told my wife that as long as I could see what was happening with my daughter's progress at school and that my daughter was OK, I would take a step back and let my daughter focus on school and my wife on being well for both herself and my daughter.  Though this hurt, I felt it was important to let my daughter feel comfortable coming to me in whatever way she wanted and rely on the fact that my wife would not be malicious about me.

I just kept as up to date as I could on her School Progress, sent messages of my love and support for her and how proud I was. As time has gone on, we have gone from messages to pictures, voice and video mails.

She is doing so well at school and outside school has such ability in the arts, these sustain me.  I am so proud of her.  From my side I will just make sure she knows that I love her more than ever, I am very proud of her and her mum is still her best friend and support.

I may not be right in my approach but it has to be better than that of my parents.  Both were affected by what happened for the rest of their lives and my mum was twisted by it.  I never spoke to my mum after that, and my dad became a bit of a hero of mine so it obviously had an impact on me as well.

# Chapter 19

I have a very good friend in the US. We have been great friends for nearly 20 years. Both of us had held senior positions covering a great deal of the senior roles in consultancies from cradle to grave of the business.

We then for 10 years worked together as a joint force with shared joint job titles. It's a big deal for anyone to do this as effectively whilst you share in any victories, any failures are joint failures.

Basically, I completely trusted my American friend on anything we did and vice versa. Whilst we had each covered all of the roles, our very distinct personalities meant together we achieved even more.

My American friend has this natural ability, where in a room, leave him for a few hours and he is everyone's friend. It is just his personality, not contrived in any way. He loves company, interaction and having fun. He also can lead easily, with people naturally liking working with him.

I am a bit more intense; I am obsessed by problem solving and solutioning. I have managed people all my life but generally they buy into my vision, my beliefs, my problem solving. I am best socialising at one to ones and small groups, as I am not really a party lover.

That is not to say in any work that we did, that only one of us could do it, we both could but we found in working through solutions, we were even better together and we were quite something at how we broke down tasks and worked on them together. It was seamless.

We virtually never disagreed on approach, although we both had strong opinions and so we were extremely good at carrying a joint vision.

We also believed in the same principles of management about how to find the right people, how to lead from the front, how to motivate and develop people, how to create something people wanted to be part of, how to make our teams solid units with everyone fighting towards the same goal.

Ultimately with good management, good selection, a real vision, a commitment to the best and to developing the team, most man management issues disappear. If everyone is fighting in the same direction, you just need to make sure the guidance is there.

We had always talked about setting up a business but it had never happened. We were so busy all the time. One night recently, my American friend said something that meant a lot to me. He said he was waiting for me to recover so that we could work together again. He had waited 7 years.

We started talking about a book I was planning on writing about teenage suicide and its causes. I had when I reconnected with friends, come across 3 whose daughters had attempted suicide.

What we discussed was whether there was anything that could be done to prevent or pre-empt this. The more we discussed it, the more we realised that this was possible, that it was something that mattered so much and that we wanted to do. This mattered to both of us personally, as we both have daughters. Additionally, the sheer scale of the problem and the fact it is endemic, meant possibilities existed to save lives, potentially a lot of lives.

A clear sign of a very good solution to a problem is whether people think; Surely, that must exist already or that is so obviously a good idea, why didn't I think of that. This is one of those ideas.

From what we initially could see, no one else out there was doing the same thing.

Whenever we broached the idea with people everyone said what a good idea it was. Now we had to think about what to do with the idea.

# Chapter 20

I had never before worked on a start-up. I mean from inception onwards. When we started, me and my American friend, had no idea what was involved. We knew we needed to develop an application for our idea but what else was involved in starting a business. It's a very different proposition, to dealing with an established business.

To start with, we got onboard a third founder, who was capable of designing, building and implementing the solution. Across the three of us we could cover all the primary roles in the company, at least in the early stages. we spent time, gaining an understanding between us of what this application would be.

After spending some time, it became clear we needed a business plan. Whilst many businesses just start up, spending time analysing what was in these business plans, we realised quite quickly was the most important task of all.

On one side, there is a mountain of things to do and understand and for me the added element of the fact we decided to incorporate in America, so suddenly I had to understand the different types of US incorporation and the very different ways in which companies are established, taxed and operated in the US.

One I will mention, is that you have to incorporate in a state and that you are subject to taxes and laws in that state. I never realised for example that one of the most popular places to incorporate is Delaware. Companies can incorporate in Delaware and unless they do business in Delaware do not have to pay business taxes there. Additionally, they have a dedicated court for issues with corporations speeding things up.

I just had never thought of this, being so used to the idea of a single tax entity, through which all tax was paid, although I had always been aware of sales taxes varying when I travelled in the US.

I also found it fascinating that you have to register as a foreign entity when you do incorporate in one state and operate in another. Sorry to digress but for me its fascinating and all my life it's been the case and I have never been aware of it.

One of the first things you have to do when you start a company is a competitive analysis. The thing I like about a detailed business plan is it guides you, to all of the things you need to show others that you know about your business (for any investment). There is a lot to investigate, find out and document but it all makes so much sense. Also, in investigating and completing the business plan it gives you so much more confidence, in the ability to achieve what you want.

So, we spent some time researching everything we could find about anyone else in this space. Once you have identified primary competitors, the process gets easier as you can look at who your competitor sees as its competition, how the technology review press compare this company against competition or who the financial overview companies and press see as the competition for those companies and you can quite quickly build a picture of who is out there.

It became clear that there was one product that had looked at and seen the same issue as we did, however it had a very different view as to what to do about it. For us we wanted both to make a difference in people's lives proactively, we wanted to try to save lives and if successful try to change the situation at a local, regional and national level to help prevent the situations that lost lives.

We have put a lot of work since, into building a business plan and there are so many variables in doing so. There is so much to it but so rewarding when doing it, and you realise why all these terms on Dragons Den and Shark Tank are so important. You just can't complete a thorough business plan without a lot of research.

Mind you, I do understand the obsession with an idea can drive People to just want to build the product and then worry about marketing it. I hadn't realised the sheer exposure you create, in doing so. I am not someone for doing something by the book but the business plan is like a guidebook for understanding your business and whether it is really viable.

We have progressed a lot and I hope I will be writing in detail about the business in future. It's strange when you are so excited about something but cannot disclose it.

# Chapter 21

Christmas is approaching as I write this. This is the longest period in my life, that I have lived alone since 1987. It has been quite a year. In some ways my previous long-term recovery helped me quite a lot.

I had been diagnosed as diabetic whilst in hospital. During the period my wife was at home afterwards, I was only eating one meal a day. I was given test strips and lancets to test my blood, which during the time I was testing was all good.

The thing was once I went to a mental health ward, they heavily encouraged me to eat three meals a day, which I stayed good and always had the diabetic choices. However, it got me back on eating 3 times a day.

Once home I did a lot of research and changed my diet quite regularly. At first being home alone, I would eat something I liked a lot, too often and put myself off it. I was also surprised to find a lot of things I really liked were diabetic friendly such as eggs, avocado, chilli, garlic and ginger. At first, I was worried I would be having plain chicken and veg for the rest of my life, just to find spices and things I could add really perked me up.

The strange thing is it got me more inventive with meals so for example for breakfast I was really into Brown Toast with olive oil, garlic, chilli and tomato passata with sprinkles of onions for breakfast and I loved it. However, I have cut down on the wholemeal bread and instead have wholemeal tortillas. Overall though I have enjoyed my food this year.

Ian being the friend that he is, asked me about Christmas and I said I had no plans.  He usually goes to his sisters but said she was busy this year.  Anyway, he suggested we got together xmas day which I agreed to.

A month or so later, I realised that on Boxing Day he is heading straight down to his sisters.  If I had known he had that option I wouldn't have said yes to Xmas day as I wouldn't have wanted to change his plans.  Ian would have realised that.  He hasn't said anything about it but another example of him being a good friend.

My sleeping has changed quite a lot.  I get a good solid amount of sleep every day but it is a bit more fragmented.  I am much more aware of when I am tired and sleep around that, which is far easier when you are home alone.

It has always been difficult to chat to my brother, as we are generally either 12 or 13 hours apart time wise and between his job, his studying for a new planned job, his family and young children and work around the house it is difficult for him to make calls.  However, we worked out when he was travelling with work, I can then sleep in blocks around that time to allow us to speak, while he is travelling between jobs.  It actually works really well.

This has been brilliant, as generally we may get maybe 2-3 calls every six months but we have been able to speak almost every week, which we probably haven't done since he has been in New Zealand some 17-18 years ago.

I have found I sleep so much better when I sleep in solid chunks and when I wake, if not sleepy just do things for a while. As soon as I feel like I am sleepy, in the slightest I will sleep again.

I still haven't had any dreams about what happened to me in those years, so assume that it actually didn't traumatise me in any way. Which is strange actually but kind of in line with how I feel about this consciously.

It's been a strange year for me and probably indicative of my age but I have seen more hospitals, blood tests, the GP etc in the last year than in any 5 previous years put together.

Strangely I am OK with this. Being aware of my diabetes and at least tracking it and dealing with what were some long-term issues (for example my gall bladder) feels like a positive thing.

When I had my double hydrocele operation, I was given the option of having spine induced anaesthetic rather than general anaesthetic. I had always wanted to be awake in an operation. Its funny when I tell people this, they find it an horrendous idea but ever since I had seen those brain operations on TV where they are operating on the brain and seeing if people can still recollect words, I was always interested in what went on during an operation.

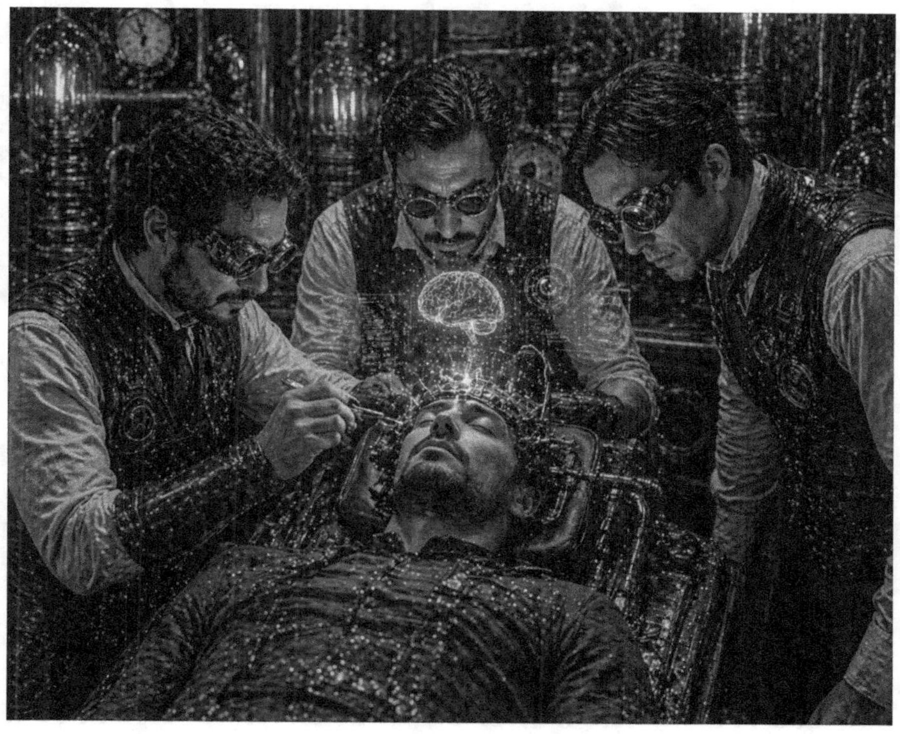

I had no idea that there were so many staff focused on the anaesthetic (4 during the operation) and the constant attention required by the anaesthetist to all sorts of factors. It was really impressive. As was the professionalism of all the staff involved in the operation. Now this may seem strange but I kind of felt sorry for these staff as it was so well done (like a formula 1 tyre change). The fact that their best work is witnessed by anaesthetised patients seems a bit sad.

Although there was one operation, I was glad I wasn't awake for. That was my recent gall bladder operation. It had to be abandoned after they couldn't get a breathing tube inserted once I was under. I have to go to a specialist unit for that operation now, though its great that they realised that there was an issue and abandoned it quickly.

I have heard a people complain about the hospital services for physical illness. Having been in hospital multiple times in the last 12 months and I was extremely ill when they discovered the issue with my gall bladder, to me the service is brilliant in all regards.

Incredible professionalism, care and food. When I compare my stays in NHS hospitals to private hospitals, I would say give me the NHS any time. Private care may give you more rapid access but I am incredibly proud of the care and treatment I have been given by the NHS, for physical care.

So, this wasn't the year I envisaged but it's been an interesting year. I look forward to the next with the hope it's a bit more straight forward so I can spend more time writing and on the start-up.

# Afterword

It's very bitter sweet.  I finally became myself again and the very reason I came back for, that all those years I thought about, were gone (within two weeks of me regaining all my faculties).

The ultimate irony, appears to be that the very act of me becoming me again, appears to be the reason they left.  Probably the extremely sudden recovery, after so long and the resultant changes may all have been overload.  Ultimately, however much I love my wife, I wouldn't want her to be unhappy and if that is what she needs then so be it.

Actually, the irony piles on, my wife ends up contacting the last people in the world, I would ever want to see and instigates me having to revisit that world almost immediately, after the first time in several years I can think clearly, where all they want me to do is take abilify.

Anyway, actually it has allowed me to get a really good understanding of what the mental health environment is like when you are not sick (though I think people were a lot sicker in the last hospital I was in).  I think I was a little worried about whether it would cause me flashbacks or trauma.  However, it was the opposite.

I was lucky to get to spend time, with some really lovely people who had just experienced some tough times and to really get to analyse the differences medication makes and its sometimes-sledgehammer approach to mental illness that can kill the mind as well as the mental illness.

I had thought about writing a book about talking to a brick wall and how to get the most from it but decided to add that in here. I never thought this lack of communication would be total and for so long. The weird thing is how we have managed to establish a way of communicating where only one side ever says anything.

Gradually though I am building a relationship with my daughter, one I couldn't have built before my recovery. Any time, in any way I can develop that I will.

It was weird writing this book, after the first book. When I had finished the first book nearly a year ago, I put the book down knowing it needed to be edited. It took me several months for me to be able to pick it up again to edit it. I just couldn't reread it. I think it was kind of raw and I needed some distance.

However, when I could reread the book and I started editing, I actually enjoyed the editing process a lot. So much so, I started writing this book the same day I finished editing the last.

Additionally, I have loved forming the start-up with my friend and our third founder. Just the chance to do something that could actually save lives. The whole process of defining a company and building a solution is really something special.

So overall it's been quite a year and when I look at it, I look positively as it also shows the roots for the future.

I love writing, it really calms my soul.  I have a feeling you haven't seen the last of me.  Assuming that you are still reading of course!

# Appendix A – Questions and Answers

All answers to questions especially on NHS teams are based on my personal experiences.  I am quite happy to answer any more questions readers have.  I will do this in batches to stop unnecessary frequent updates to the book.

1.  **In relation to your mind how have you changed in the year since the recovery from brain damage?**

Surprisingly little.  In most regards I am the same as I was **before** I was ill in 2015.  I have the same facets to my character.  Still quite determined, still very inquisitive, still love films and TV drama and interacting with friends, still very focused.

Some of these things surprise me, as with so long not being able to do these things, I am not sure why these traits have lasted, though I am glad that they have.  They came back quite suddenly.  As a layman's guess I would guess that when the neurons finally connected, they connected to these traits which have lay dormant.

As discussed before loads of little changes though.  My favourite is my increased ability at dealing with the big situations.  Specifically, to let things go and move on.  My memory of films and TV shows is not as good as it was.  Surprisingly everything else I seem to have good recall.

In fact, I think my general recall is better than it was.  It's difficult to know, as before my mind would be full of work both at work and when travelling, so maybe there is just more room for things.

## 2.   Have you had any after affects from the recovery?

I haven't had a single bad dream (that I remember!). No flashbacks. No feelings of being trapped in myself, no worries about whether I could think.  Still a niggle about whether this clarity will stay but just a niggle and nothing that has happened indicates that.

## 3.   Did going back into a mental hospital setting cause you any issues?

No, whilst I was there, I didn't experience any increased or changed memories regarding 2015.  Nothing more came back to me; I didn't have any sense of Déjà Vu or anything like that.  This actually surprised me.  I really thought it may trigger memories or something.

I had been worried it may cause me some form of flashbacks or that people may get under my skin reminding me of 2015.

It's a strange thing to say but I enjoyed the experience.  It allowed me to write this book, I met some really interesting people and it's surprising just how nice most of them are.

I had enjoyable conversations with them and formed quite close bonds with them while I was there.  I even miss them a little.  People in those situations are surprisingly open and honest and that is refreshing.

You really get a sense that anyone is only a few steps away from the situation.  You are also left in no doubt as to the sheer power of these medications and the massive impact it has on people's personalities and confidence.

Overall if anything this has helped me close the book on a lot of my concerns re mental health hospitals.  I have one more task to do, which I have avoided and that is to look at the several hundred pages of notes from the Mental Health Units covering my initial stay in 2015.  Some books you don't want to open.  I look forward to it, in the same way people in a horror film look forward to entering a cellar.

**4.  Are you suggesting in your book that the Crisis team is incompetent or abusive of power?**

I am not saying that all of the team are but at the same time, it's not just one or two staff that abuse the positions they hold.  I think it's a bit of a combination of both.  Some staff both abuse their position and I believe are incompetent.

Some of the team seem to struggle to do their jobs and it seems to invite at least a quorum of people who have a power complex. Simply put they seem to enjoy the power they wield over people. Additionally, some of these people would not have the intelligence to hold equivalent jobs in the police or study for medical positions.

Some of the teams are genuine, they honestly evaluate the situation and not trying to assert themselves over the vulnerable.

The falsehoods that are written by some of the team, which are in alignment with an outcome they wish to see are shocking and done with such abandon, that they obviously believe they will never get caught. They threaten people with outcomes to gain compliance and have powers to force the issue, that only a few in the country hold.

I am fully aware that the teams have a very difficult job in many situations and people genuinely in crisis need to be dealt with quickly to protect themselves and others. I am sure many of the teams use their powers wisely and appropriately.

The issue here is a number of the team wield that power inappropriately and enjoy doing it just a little too much to not be worried about these people dealing with vulnerable people. There should always be checks and balances and making sure these people are fit and proper to do this job is one of them,

## 5. What are you saying about the doctors in the mental health unit?

Firstly, the person who seemed to make the most sense when dealing with situations, was the consultant in charge. My conversations with the consultant were plain and dealt with the reality of the situation and the consultant told me plainly what their thinking was. So overall with the consultant I knew what was going on. An accurate record was kept, it was clear someone recorded in notes what was said.

My issue is that this isn't the case on the Admissions and Discharge Documents.  There is an assumption that statements made by the Crisis team can be cut and pasted as though it was said to the doctor (often done without attribution where the crisis team recorded the same comment and where that was the only time the subject was discussed).  In a number of cases things were just made up and ended up in dozens of documents.

What goes into those reports is what the doctor chooses to record so my own comments were highly distorted and many things were just not said in the documents or the opposite of what I had said.

Comments that are easily proven false and were just plain silly like me thinking my car was stolen, were placed in order to support an earlier conclusion made by the crisis team.

**6.  So, what do you believe should be done about the Crisis team and the Mental Health Unit?**

I have compiled and submitted my views on this for the unit I was on and they are simple but far reaching: -

Record all key meetings and allow the patient to do the same.  This eliminates 99% of the opportunity for falsehoods, that currently exist in creating the document, especially where the patient has no proof as they are told not to record, they are not given copies of the documents and they may well be heavily medicated so struggle both with recall and expression.

Ensure that patients are explicitly aware of those things not discussed in the meeting but put in the doctors' documents.  It was only in my meetings with the consultant was I ever told what was going on and what they were thinking.

Give copies of all clinical notes to patient or family if the person cannot process, so it is clear what is being said and the patient is informed.  I was given nothing apart from a do you understand document, which I was given 6 days in.

I read 45 pages of 72-hour care plans under GDPR, none of which I was shown for example whilst in the hospital.

Record and retain video of the inside of the Nurses station.  People are locked in that room and often no staff are on the wards. Overnight that can be for prolonged periods of time, with all staff in the nurse's station which makes me question, the accuracy of the "constant checks" that are performed on patients

Record and retain video of the outside of the Nurses station.  Nurses leave people waiting deliberately, as long as they can.  During the day it was not uncommon to see a queue of people waiting outside for anyone to come out.

Put a focus on mental wellness.  For a mental health ward, the focus is on sustenance, measurement, hygiene and medication.  All of the people I spoke to had real issues that just were not being addressed e.g., nowhere to live when they left care, no money and no understanding of how to apply for benefits especially from inside. There should be a much higher volunteer presence helping people to address their issues and offering someone to talk to.  The advocate program doesn't seem to work as in my 11 days I didn't hear of an advocate visiting the ward and some long-term patients didn't know what an advocate was and how they could help.

## 7.   Why didn't your wife tell you what she was doing?

My wife was very gentle.  As I said I don't remember ever raising my voice and we never argued.  When I was gone, she absorbed what happened to me and got on with things.  I am not sure that meant that she really coped however.

She made a real point of telling me a few days before that she couldn't stand conflict or arguments. It was a story about work.  I can't help feeling that was for me.

I think that she was either worried I would convince her to come back or she was scared it would be raised voices and I am not sure she could cope with that.

## 8.   Why have you invested so much time digging into your Mental Health Stay?  You can't get the time back

This is a very interesting question.  When I was about 10.  I found two older kids beating up my friend and I jumped in to try to get them to stop.  My friend managed to escape, although he then ran off, which I do understand.  We met for a drink several years ago and he felt compelled to apologize for this.  I was never a fighter and got beaten up quite badly.  I knew going in, that would happen.

However, I have had a lifelong objection to bullies.  At work this translated to intellectual bullies.  When I saw the mental health trust openly bully me (and enjoy it), It riled me.  When I saw that this continued into the hospital (for example with the threat of sectioning), this made me sit up.

At first, I was extremely conscious of the fact that I was well, yet still they were pushing as though I wasn't.   If I had given in and taken the medication, I would have been medicated.   They could have recorded me as treated.   I would have been badly affected cognitively and not had the memories or been able to represent myself.

Although I could stand up for myself, with the issues that I had with the hospital, it was those who were vulnerable, who were ill, that I became concerned for.   How can they stand up for themselves?   Who would believe them if they did?

I know being reasonably intelligent all my life and successful, that after being ill, even only once, every authority I dealt with after that treated me as though I was still ill and that my complaint related to that illness.   I want the trust to take accountability.

9.   **What do you foresee in regards to your relationship with your daughter?**

I will forever, just be there for her and make it clear to her how much I love her and how proud I am.   I will be in her life as much as she is comfortable to let me and will go at her pace, in building our relationship.

I am very happy that now that I get to hear her voice and see video clips.   I missed that terribly.   Knowing she is well and doing well is a big deal for me.

## 10. What about your wife?

As I don't know her reasons for what she chose to do, what made her leave and as we don't talk, I am limited.  From my side she was the love of my life.  What I have decided is to let things be.

Everyone deserves happiness.  If for whatever reason she could not find that with me, then she needs to find her happiness.  For many years I wasn't really there and that must have left a vacuum in her life.